AF279174

pray

a word for

strength

connecting to God one word
at a time

editors of guideposts

 Guideposts

A Gift from Guideposts

Thank you for your purchase! We appreciate your support and want to express our gratitude with a special gift just for you.

Dive into *Spirit Lifters*, a complimentary booklet that will fortify your faith and offer solace during challenging moments. It contains 31 carefully selected verses from scripture that will soothe your soul and uplift your spirit.

Please use the QR code or go to **guideposts.org/spiritlifters** to download.

Pray a Word for Strength

Published by Guideposts
100 Reserve Road, Suite E200
Danbury, CT 06810
Guideposts.org

ISBN 978-1-961251-15-1 (hardcover)
ISBN 978-1-961251-16-8 (softcover)
ISBN 978-1-961251-17-5 (ebook)

Cover and interior design by Serena Fox, Bean Inc.
Cover photo © Shutterstock: Ilolab
Typeset by Aptara, Inc.

Printed and bound in the United States of America
$PrintCode

Do you not know? Have you not heard?
The Lord is the everlasting God, the Creator of
the ends of the earth. He will not grow tired
or weary, and his understanding no one can
fathom. He gives strength to the weary
and increases the power of the weak.
—Isaiah 40:28–29 (NIV)

Introduction

Strength. How many of us have watched as a friend or acquaintance dealt with a challenging situation and thought to ourselves, *If only I could be so strong*? It's almost as if some of us consider strength a perpetual state of mind or a hereditary trait that never fluctuates. But it's altogether different than that. It doesn't simply happen. Just as we build up muscle mass with consistent physical training, our spiritual strength requires steady immersion in prayer and the Bible to thrive.

As believers, our source of strength is God. Dwight L. Moody put it this way: "Real, true faith is man's weakness leaning on God's strength." God's limitless might is available to us everywhere and always. Like all of His attributes, it is unshakable and unfailing.

When David entered the battlefield to face off against Goliath, his courage was rooted in his deep faith in God. He brought five stones to accomplish a task that to most seemed impossible, even foolhardy. Yet he only needed to sling one rock at the giant. It hit its mark perfectly, defeating Goliath. David's trust and God's hand formed an invincible duo.

The same holds true when we move forward in faith. Paul wrote in his letter to the Philippians, verse 4:13 (NKJV), "I can do all things through Christ who strengthens me."

Jesus understands our needs and provides us strength in ways that fit us as individuals and every unique situation we encounter. He might offer us His strength through a friend's support or a Bible verse that speaks directly to our challenge—or even a word to meditate on throughout the day. Words carry power. When we focus on a specific word, we can gain God's strength through it.

This empowering collection is undated, providing you the freedom to enjoy it at your own pace. An inspiring prayer and a page of scripture accompany each devotion as you delve into a deeper, more intimate experience of God's presence in your life. Space is offered for recording thoughts, prayer requests, or whatever you wish. As you reflect on each encouraging devotion, apply it to your life. And be strong and courageous, for God will be with you wherever you go.

—Heidi Gaul

warm-up

My husband teaches and trains people to move from the couch to running a 5K race. Every session begins with a warm-up. He takes them through a series of gentle stretches to warm up their muscles, preparing their bodies for what's to come.

Prayer is my spiritual warm-up. When I take the time to present myself before Jesus, shedding the chaos of whatever's distracting me, I move into a place of deeper connection with Him and prepare my soul for the day to come. The more time I take to warm up my spiritual muscles in His presence, the more apt I am to be like John in the book of Revelation: able to hear the Lord's voice like a trumpet, regardless of how noisy my world is.

—Claire McGarry

Lord of Peace, quiet my heart so I hear Your voice no matter how loudly or softly You speak. Amen.

Words to Pray On

On the Lord's Day I was in the Spirit, and I heard
behind me a loud voice like a trumpet.

—Revelation 1:10 (NIV)

The Lord will indeed give what is good, and our land
will yield its harvest. Righteousness goes before him
and prepares the way for his steps.

—Psalm 85:12–13 (NIV)

And it will be said: "Build up, build up, prepare the
road! Remove the obstacles out of the way of my
people."

—Isaiah 57:14 (NIV)

reach

"Let's ride bikes across the Brooklyn Bridge," I said. It sounded like a good way to spend a muggy New York day.

By the time we biked into Brooklyn, cruised a few miles along the waterfront, then circled back to ascend the looping incline onto the borough's famous bridge, I was spent. I pedaled at a snail's pace.

And then I felt it. The strong, stabilizing boost of my husband's hand on my back offered hope that we might actually reach Manhattan before the end of the calendar year. He gave my bicycle seat a push, caught up to me, and then reached over, placing his hand on my back again—this time leaving it there and cycling alongside me.

God's like that, isn't He? When we're at our weakest, He reaches into our story, and with a strong, stabilizing hand He propels us on. I love Him for that.

—Laurie Davies

Jesus, thank You that Your strength is on display most powerfully when we are weak. Remind us to call upon Your mighty name. Amen.

Words to Pray On

But he said to me, "My grace is sufficient for you, for my power is made perfect in weakness." Therefore I will boast all the more gladly about my weaknesses, so that Christ's power may rest on me. That is why, for Christ's sake, I delight in weaknesses, in insults, in hardships, in persecutions, in difficulties. For when I am weak, then I am strong.

—2 Corinthians 12:9–10 (NIV)

I will strengthen Judah and save the tribes of Joseph. I will restore them because I have compassion on them. They will be as though I had not rejected them, for I am the Lord their God and I will answer them.

—Zechariah 10:6 (NIV)

They realized that this work had been done with the help of our God.

—Nehemiah 6:16 (NIV)

clutter

I'm cleaning out the basement. Some of the "treasures" I've collected over the years I can sell, and a few I'll donate. A large part of the accumulation comprises broken things I should have tossed in the trash long ago.

This mess is much like the clutter that fills my mind. Many of my preoccupations don't even belong in my thoughts, like situations and people I can't fix, and emotional baggage I hang on to.

Getting rid of mental clutter and worries is an ongoing process for me. Long after I've completed my basement project, I'll still be handing Jesus my emotional "stuff" and asking Him what I should hold on to and what to let go. And He will continue guiding me, building my trust in Him as He clears out the clutter.

—Heidi Gaul

Jesus, help me discern the thoughts You desire for me as You declutter my mind. Amen.

Words to Pray On

So do not worry, saying, "What shall we eat?" or
"What shall we drink?" or "What shall we wear?"
For the pagans run after all these things, and your
heavenly Father knows that you need them. But seek
first his kingdom and his righteousness, and all these
things will be given to you as well. Therefore do not
worry about tomorrow, for tomorrow will worry about
itself. Each day has enough trouble of its own.

—Matthew 6:31–34 (NIV)

I consider everything a loss because of the surpassing
worth of knowing Christ Jesus my Lord, for whose
sake I have lost all things. I consider them garbage,
that I may gain Christ and be found in him.

—Philippians 3:8–9 (NIV)

adopted

When my mother died of cancer at the age of 49, it seemed life would never be the same without her. My five siblings splintered apart, and my devastated dad sold the house and moved to another state. Six months later, he got a call.

Lilly had just lost both of her adoptive parents and only now felt free to reach out. An only child, she was the daughter given up by my mother long ago, unbeknownst to any of us. Our broken family flew to Atlanta to meet her, and we cried looking at the very image of my mom, young and well. We squeezed her tightly, holding on for dear life. She wept with joy for the family she never knew she had.

Children of God are much the same. We are separated, seemingly alone. But if we reach out, we are returned to the family that was always there.

—Kimberly Shumate

Father, I pray for the strength of family—in every goodbye, and in every hello. Thank You for adopting me into Your loving family. Amen.

Words to Pray On

God decided in advance to adopt us into his own family by bringing us to himself through Jesus Christ. This is what he wanted to do, and it gave him great pleasure. So we praise God for the glorious grace he has poured out on us who belong to his dear Son.

—Ephesians 1:5–6 (NLT)

"I will be a Father to you, and you will be my sons and daughters," says the Lord Almighty.

—2 Corinthians 6:18 (NIV)

Consequently, you are no longer foreigners and strangers, but fellow citizens with God's people and also members of his household, built on the foundation of the apostles and prophets, with Christ Jesus himself as the chief cornerstone.

—Ephesians 2:19–20 (NIV)

through

We all face dark valleys in life. For me, cancer was a valley that terrified me. I did not want to walk through it; I just wanted to run away or give up. At the same time, I couldn't quit or pretend. I had choices to make and children to raise. I struggled to know which treatment to choose, and everything ahead was a scary unknown.

When a friend pointed me to Isaiah, the word *through* jumped off the page. Each day, I would recite Isaiah 43:2 (see opposite page) and remind myself to breathe. From that point on, with every test, every step, I would breathe in and remember: "God is my Through." Then I'd breathe out and let go of a little more of the fear.

God is our Through. He walks us through every struggle, every dark valley, and every hard day. He is how we keep going.

—Amy Wallace

Lord, You alone are my Through. Carry me through the hard places today. Amen.

Words to Pray On

When you go through deep waters, I will be with you. When you go through rivers of difficulty, you will not drown. When you walk through the fire of oppression, you will not be burned up; the flames will not consume you.

—Isaiah 43:2 (NLT)

Even when I walk through the darkest valley, I will not be afraid, for you are close beside me. Your rod and your staff protect and comfort me.

—Psalm 23:4 (NLT)

Yes, I am the gate. Those who come in through me will be saved. They will come and go freely and will find good pastures.

—John 10:9 (NLT)

persimmons

One November, I visited a cemetery where a relative is buried. The air told me of nuts and fallen leaves and the coming winter. Nearby, persimmons clung to a tree and others littered the ground.

Wild American persimmons are a unique fruit: They're not ready to eat until cold weather. They're a burnt orange color and so sweet when ripe. Pioneers used them for puddings, breads, and beer. But before ripening, they're highly astringent. To echo Ecclesiastes, there is a time to eat persimmons and a time to not eat persimmons! I ate some that day, and they were delicious—nothing like the ones in the grocery store.

Their unusual quality of being inedible until ripe reminds me of how sometimes we have to wait for a blessing to come at its appointed time: a baby, a promotion, a job, better health, or a passing. There's a time for everything, and everything is sweeter in its time.

—Nancy Schrock

Lord, help me to remember that strength comes in waiting for Your appointed times.

Words to Pray On

There is a time for everything, and a season for every activity under the heavens.

—Ecclesiastes 3:1 (NIV)

The Lord will open the heavens, the storehouse of his bounty, to send rain on your land in season and to bless all the work of your hands.

—Deuteronomy 28:12 (NIV)

Blessed is the one…whose delight is in the law of the Lord, and who meditates on his law day and night. That person is like a tree planted by streams of water, which yields its fruit in season and whose leaf does not wither—whatever they do prospers.

—Psalm 1:1–3 (NIV)

love

Following hip replacement surgery, I was instructed to do leg-strengthening exercises—twenty leg lifts for each leg, twice each day, for a whole year. I wanted my legs to get stronger, but how could I faithfully do all those boring exercises?

I could do them during my husband's yoga classes, but that was only twice per week. Then I thought of my prayer list—the friends and loved ones I tried to pray for regularly. Could I combine my exercises with praying for their specific situations?

I decided to trust that God knows everyone's needs much better than I do. I closed my eyes. I counted my first leg lift. "One…" I pictured one friend surrounded by God's love. "Two…" I pictured my neighbors surrounded by God's love. "Three…" Each day, as I counted the final leg lift, I felt God's love embracing me.

—Leanne Jackson

Dear Lord, may I share Your love faithfully, every day. Amen.

Words to Pray On

A new command I give you: Love one another. As I have loved you, so must you love one another. By this everyone will know that you are my disciples, if you love one another.

—John 13:34–35 (NIV)

Be devoted to one another in love. Honor one another above yourselves.

—Romans 12:10 (NIV)

How priceless is your unfailing love, O God! People take refuge in the shadow of your wings.

—Psalm 36:7 (NIV)

A friend loves at all times, and a brother is born for a time of adversity.

—Proverbs 17:17 (NIV)

everywhere

I'm excited and scared to move out of state soon.

Last summer, I felt led to buy a house in another city. After many failed offers, I gave up. Then I applied for a great job there and got it. I submitted another home contract and the owner picked me, even though I had the lowest bid. Definitely God's provision.

Still, I've been in the same place for almost 20 years. It hurts to pull up roots that deep. Deuteronomy 31:8 (see opposite page) reminded me that God had gone before me by sending a friend to live there a year ago. I know that God will be with me to help me adjust and grow new roots.

Have you ever feared change? Wherever God leads you, He is creating circumstances for your good and His glory. He won't forget your new address. He's already there. God is everywhere.

—Joanna Eccles

Dear God, thank You for going before us to make a way and being with us every day. Amen.

Words to Pray On

And the Lord, He is the One who goes before you.
He will be with you, He will not leave you nor forsake
you; do not fear nor be dismayed.

—Deuteronomy 31:8 (NKJV)

Not that I speak in regard to need, for I have learned
in whatever state I am, to be content: I know how to
be abased, and I know how to abound. Everywhere
and in all things I have learned both to be full and to
be hungry, both to abound and to suffer need. I can
do all things through Christ who strengthens me.

—Philippians 4:11–13 (NKJV)

surrender

My four-year-old grandson loves to help. When there's a package on the front porch to bring in, he's right there wanting to bring it in for me. Problem is, many times the packages are too heavy for him to carry. He'll give it his best try, really wanting to be helpful. But then he'll surrender and say, "You need to do it, Nana. It's too heavy for me." I hear you, buddy.

Jesus knew as well that the burden the religious leaders were putting on the people of Israel was too heavy for them to carry. So many rules, so much pressure to keep all the laws. That's why He encouraged His followers to surrender their burden to Him, to take *His* yoke upon them. His burden is light, He said. His yoke is easy. He boiled the law down to just two things: Love God, love others. That's something even a child can do.

—Stephanie Reeves

Lord, thank You for understanding that we just can't carry the weight of our own salvation. I surrender my efforts to You. I surrender the idea that I have to earn Your favor. What a relief! In Your name I pray. Amen.

Words to Pray On

Come to me, all you who are weary and burdened, and I will give you rest. Take my yoke upon you and learn from me, for I am gentle and humble in heart, and you will find rest for your souls. For my yoke is easy and my burden is light.

—Matthew 11:28–30 (NIV)

Cast all your anxiety on him because he cares for you.

—1 Peter 5:7 (NIV)

For there is no distinction between Jew and Greek; for the same Lord is Lord of all, bestowing his riches on all who call on him. For "everyone who calls on the name of the Lord will be saved."

—Romans 10:12–13 (ESV)

burdened

When my children were toddlers, I attended a young mother's Bible study where once a week, for 2 hours, volunteers cared for the children in another room while the moms talked, laughed, studied the Bible, and prayed together. One morning the group leader asked us how we felt. One woman replied, "Like a beast of burden." We all laughed in mutual understanding.

When Jesus calls burdened people to come to Him, it's a general call to us all, for we all carry loads that are too heavy to bear alone. The mother who came in heavy seemed to feel lighter after her confession. Why? Because we understood—she wasn't alone. And what about the volunteers who allowed us to experience weekly mom-breathers? They sacrificed their time so we could enjoy the blessing of fellowship. They were burden-lifters, like Jesus.

—Grace Assante

Lord, as You care for me, help me to have eyes, ears, hands, and feet to care for others. Amen.

Words to Pray On

But I call to God, and the Lord will save me. Evening and morning and at noon I utter my complaint and moan, and he hears my voice. He redeems my soul in safety from the battle that I wage. . . . Cast your burden on the Lord, and he will sustain you; he will never permit the righteous to be moved.

—Psalm 55:16–18, 22 (ESV)

For I do not mean that others should be eased and you burdened, but that as a matter of fairness your abundance at the present time should supply their need, so that their abundance may supply your need, that there may be fairness.

—2 Corinthians 8:13–14 (ESV)

letter

Weeping family members stood in the hospital room. The time drew near for my father's move to heaven—a place he confidently believed was his eternal destination.

My siblings and I took turns stepping close to Dad's bedside to verbalize our goodbyes. Tears flowed freely, as did our final words to him.

"Dad, what I'll miss most is you not being able to send me letters from heaven," I choked out when my turn came. Dad had regularly written letters to me my entire adult life. I didn't realize how much they meant until I faced never receiving any again.

One Bible verse, 2 Corinthians 3:3 (see opposite page), offers me great comfort in Dad's earthly absence. While I can't receive letters from him anymore, I can, as Paul noted, be a living letter to those around me. I pray Dad is looking down approvingly from heaven on my letter to the world about Jesus.

—Alice H. Murray

Dear God, help me to be a living letter, conveying my faith in Jesus to all those with whom I have contact. Amen.

Words to Pray On

You yourselves are our letter, written on our hearts, known and read by everyone. You show that you are a letter from Christ, the result of our ministry, written not with ink but with the Spirit of the living God, not on tablets of stone but on tablets of human hearts.

—2 Corinthians 3:2–3 (NIV)

For some say, "His letters are weighty and forceful, but in person he is unimpressive and his speaking amounts to nothing." Such people should realize that what we are in our letters when we are absent, we will be in our actions when we are present.

—2 Corinthians 10:10–11 (NIV)

anxiety

Every morning, a male bluebird perches in front of my husband's rearview mirror and sees *him*. Another bluebird. A threat to his nest tucked in the tree above. He pecks the foul fowl until his head is nearly smashed flat and his beak resembles the blunt end of a hammer. He doesn't realize he's fighting his own reflection.

Anxiety is a liar. It tells us that because we *feel* a certain way, it must be so. It plays upon our emotions and leads us to believe our troubles are insurmountable and our circumstances are hopeless.

The good news is that when our fears seem like an impossible obstacle, God is greater. He is truth. He is the constant in a world of chaos. We need only carry our anxiety to Him. The same hands that opened and bled for us are big enough to carry our worries too.

—Tara Johnson

Lord, thank You for lifting the fears that threaten to overwhelm my heart.

Words to Pray On

Cast all your anxiety on him because he cares for you.
—1 Peter 5:7 (NIV)

When I said, "My foot is slipping," your unfailing love, LORD, supported me. When anxiety was great within me, your consolation brought me joy.
—Psalm 94:18–19 (NIV)

Cast your cares on the LORD and he will sustain you; he will never let the righteous be shaken.
—Psalm 55:22 (NIV)

grateful

Last year I was diagnosed with shingles. It was the worst pain that I have ever had to endure. I found myself struggling with depression and could not find any peace.

As I was crying out to God one day, I remembered something my mentor had told me to do when I was going through a hard time. She told me to make a list each morning of at least five things that I was grateful for. Then at night, make another list with five different things.

I was amazed at how that simple exercise changed my attitude about my situation. Now I was focused on all that God had blessed me with, instead of my health issues. Then I was able to find peace.

—Amanda Pennock

God, help me to always give thanks to You in all circumstances, and to be grateful for all You have done for me.

Words to Pray On

Give thanks in all circumstances; for this is the will of God in Christ Jesus for you.

—1 Thessalonians 5:18 (ESV)

Shout for joy to the Lord, all the earth. Worship the Lord with gladness; come before him with joyful songs. Know that the Lord is God. It is he who made us, and we are his; we are his people, the sheep of his pasture. Enter his gates with thanksgiving and his courts with praise; give thanks to him and praise his name. For the Lord is good and his love endures forever; his faithfulness continues through all generations.

—Psalm 100:1–5 (NIV)

enough

I'd stared at my computer for almost 2 hours. I typed a word, then deleted it. I scavenged for a profound thought worth committing to print. But nothing came. I sighed, glancing out the window at the rapidly accumulating snowfall. What I really wanted was to curl up with a book and a mug of hot cocoa. But it was a weekday. I should be busy, productive, useful...Even though I was ahead of schedule for the projects I was working on, I felt I could accomplish more. I could acquire more. I could *be* more.

That's when I sensed God whisper, *Enough.* I stopped and refocused my attention from my computer screen to the fluffy flakes performing a frosty ballet outside my window. Right now, what I'd accomplished was enough. What I possessed was enough. God was enough—and so was I.

—Vicki Kuyper

Lord, teach me when to strive, when to be still, and how to find rest in the beauty of "enough." Amen.

Words to Pray On

Why is everyone hungry for more? "More, more,"
they say. "More, more." I have God's more-than-
enough, more joy in one ordinary day than they get in
all their shopping sprees.

—Psalm 4:6–7 (MSG)

"Test me in this," says the Lord Almighty, "and see
if I will not throw open the floodgates of heaven and
pour out so much blessing that there will not be room
enough to store it."

—Malachi 3:10 (NIV)

Philip said, "Lord, show us the Father and that will be
enough for us."

—John 14:8 (NIV)

We can be tired, weary, and emotionally distraught, but after spending time alone with God, we find that He injects into our bodies energy, power, and strength.
—Charles Stanley

identity

We define ourselves by our culture, our family heritage, our language, our race, our jobs, and our faith, among other things. All of these pieces form us and make up our identity. But what if we are also identified as outcast or shamed? What if we are misunderstood?

Jesus went out of his way to speak to the Samaritan woman at the well, and he broke all sorts of taboos in doing so. He spoke respectfully, offered her living water, and showed tremendous compassion in speaking to someone who was despised and left out.

Jesus saw her and spoke life to her. If Jesus had not seen her, perhaps she would have continued living on the outskirts of society. He helped her reclaim her identity as a woman of worth, as beloved, and belonging to Him. The same identity also applies to us: beloved.

—Prasanta Verma

Dear Lord, please help me to see with Your eyes those around me who are identified as outcast and forgotten. Thank You that You identify us as beloved by You. Amen.

Words to Pray On

The Samaritan woman said to him, "You are a Jew and I am a Samaritan woman. How can you ask me for a drink?" (For Jews do not associate with Samaritans.)
—John 4:9 (NIV)

Let the beloved of the Lord rest secure in him, for he shields him all day long, and the one the Lord loves rests between his shoulders.
—Deuteronomy 33:12 (NIV)

"But I will restore you to health and heal your wounds," declares the Lord, "because you are called an outcast, Zion for whom no one cares."
—Jeremiah 30:17 (NIV)

steadfast

When we say that someone is steadfast, we ascribe to them the qualities of being faithful, dependable, unwavering, and loyal.

Several years ago, God brought Charlie into our lives. He was a young puppy with an injured hind leg. Sadly, I didn't want an injured, handicapped dog, but my wife and daughter shamed me into adopting Charlie. After I said yes, God changed my hard heart; I fell in love with Charlie, and he quickly became my shadow. If I was taking a shower, he'd wait on the bath mat for me to finish. If I was away on a trip, Charlie would lie with his eyes focused on the front door awaiting my return. Charlie was steadfast in his love and devotion to me. He was a daily reminder of God's love and faithfulness in my daily life.

—Dale R. Yancy

Dear Lord, apart from Your steadfast love, I don't know where I would be. I take comfort in Your love for me, knowing that it never ceases. Amen.

Words to Pray On

You have led in your steadfast love the people whom you have redeemed; you have guided them by your strength to your holy abode.

—Exodus 15:13 (ESV)

O LORD, God of Israel, there is no God like you, in heaven or on earth, keeping covenant and showing steadfast love to your servants who walk before you with all their heart.

—2 Chronicles 6:14 (ESV)

Give thanks to the LORD, for he is good, for his steadfast love endures forever. Give thanks to the God of gods, for his steadfast love endures forever. Give thanks to the Lord of lords, for his steadfast love endures forever.

—Psalm 136:1–3 (ESV)

cling

Along the waterline of the channel islands near my home, sea stars (starfish) cling to the slick, briny rocks as the tides rise and fall, waves pounding relentlessly. Delicately painted in hues of cinnamon, berry, and gold, they seem almost decorative. But though you can't see it, these muscular creatures are working hard, gripping tight to the surface of the rocks, and reaching with tentacled arms to grasp what they need for survival.

When life goes according to plan, I feel like I can manage just fine on my own. But when waves of hardship and loss pummel, threatening to pull me under, I reach out and cling desperately to Jesus, my rock. He never pushes me away; He invites me to come close to the Father and rely on Him for everything I need.

—Leslie McLeod

Lord, You didn't design me to function well alone. Thank You for the needs that drive me ever closer to You, where I am forever loved and cared for and safe.

Words to Pray On

Love must be sincere. Hate what is evil; cling to what is good.

—Romans 12:9 (NIV)

At this they wept aloud again. Then Orpah kissed her mother-in-law goodbye, but Ruth clung to her. "Look," said Naomi, "your sister-in-law is going back to her people and her gods. Go back with her." But Ruth replied, "Don't urge me to leave you or to turn back from you. Where you go I will go, and where you stay I will stay."

—Ruth 1:14–16 (NIV)

Jesus said to her, "Mary!" She turned and said to Him, "Rabboni!" (which is to say, Teacher). Jesus said to her, "Do not cling to Me, for I have not yet ascended to My Father; but go to My brethren and say to them, 'I am ascending to My Father and your Father, and to My God and your God.'"

—John 20:16–17 (NKJV)

liberated

"To catch a raccoon, you don't need a trap; just a hole and something shiny." As someone who'd grown up in the woods, I was skeptical, having ethically trapped opossums, groundhogs, squirrels, and raccoons. However, raccoons are intelligent and can be especially challenging to bait and capture with the best traps.

Grinning, the older man explained just how this unbelievable trapping method worked. A raccoon would fit its hand into a hole to grab a shiny object and become trapped by its clenched fist. They can escape at any time by releasing the treasure, but they refuse, clinging to the very trap that keeps them in bondage, refusing the liberation right in front of them.

How often do we ignore our liberation in Jesus, becoming the source of our bondage? As you pray the word *liberated*, imagine Jesus opening your clenched fist, freeing you from past hurts, future worries, and present confusion. Jesus is the truth, and He wants to set you free.

—AJ Smith

Jesus, You are the truth, and in You I have liberation. Help me to embrace the liberation You've made available.

Words to Pray On

Jesus said to the people who believed in him, "You are truly my disciples if you remain faithful to my teachings. And you will know the truth, and the truth will set you free."

—John 8:31–32 (NLT)

How can I know all the sins lurking in my heart? Cleanse me from these hidden faults. Keep your servant from deliberate sins! Don't let them control me. Then I will be free of guilt and innocent of great sin.

—Psalm 19:12–13 (NLT)

Thank God! Once you were slaves of sin, but now you wholeheartedly obey this teaching we have given you. Now you are free from your slavery to sin, and you have become slaves to righteous living.

—Romans 6:17–18 (NLT)

knowledge

Reading an article listing what to clean in one's home, I was surprised to see "filter on the dishwasher." The article stated that a dirty screen could send debris back to the dishes. I never realized this part required my attention. Removing the offender, I faced an accumulation of dirt and grease. I worked with soap and a brush to remove the muck. I was surprised to see my dishes sparkle. With this knowledge, I will place it on my ongoing to-do list.

I would like to think my life is squeaky clean; however, I do not pay attention to my personal gunk. It accumulates. I ignore. In prayer I can ask for knowledge of my offenses. Then God can work on my heart to change.

—Loraine McElhaney

Father God, give me knowledge of when I hurt people or You. Please show me how to change.

Words to Pray On

For the Lᴏʀᴅ gives wisdom; from his mouth come knowledge and understanding.
—Proverbs 2:6 (NIV)

The fear of the Lᴏʀᴅ is the beginning of knowledge, but fools despise wisdom and instruction.
—Proverbs 1:7 (NIV)

Now to each one the manifestation of the Spirit is given for the common good. To one there is given through the Spirit a message of wisdom, to another a message of knowledge by means of the same Spirit, to another faith by the same Spirit, to another gifts of the healing by that one Spirit.
—1 Corinthians 12:7–9 (NIV)

want

When David was diagnosed with autism, I shared his mother Rachel's sense of relief. At last, a diagnosis. As their neighbor, I had watched David develop into a charming but slightly befuddled three-year-old. His alternating silence, repetitive verbalizations, and inability to keep eye contact were part of a larger array of symptoms on the spectrum. I took comfort in knowing he would receive professional assistance.

Now would begin the hard work of placing David in the right educational framework and finding the right tools to help him advance, all without putting pressure on him to meet milestones that other kids his age might accomplish with ease.

Mothers are often only as happy as their unhappiest child. While it was hard to determine what David wanted for himself, I realized that what Rachel wanted was now within reach: the chance to watch him grow and flourish into a joyful young man.

—Miriam Green

Please, God, help all our children learn to value themselves, to be self-sufficient and autonomous, to be free from tension and worry, live peaceful lives, and feel a sense of determination.

Words to Pray On

The LORD is my shepherd; I shall not want. He makes me to lie down in green pastures; He leads me beside the still waters. He restores my soul; He leads me in the paths of righteousness for His name's sake.

—Psalm 23:1–3 (NKJV)

Oh, taste and see that the LORD is good; blessed is the man who trusts in Him! Oh, fear the LORD, you His saints! There is no want to those who fear Him.

—Psalm 34:8–9 (NKJV)

Many are the plans in a person's heart, but it is the LORD's purpose that prevails.

—Proverbs 19:21 (NIV)

wonderful

I hid my arm as I stepped into the sanctuary. I was born with half of my right arm, and it doesn't normally bother me. But surrounded by dozens of new people, I wished I could disappear into the Sunday morning crowd.

A man turned to shake my hand, then frowned. He pointed to my empty shirt sleeve. "What happened?"

"I was born with one arm."

"Oh." He turned to greet someone else.

When people stare, I can be tempted to feel like my arm is all they see. And maybe it is. But that's OK, because my arm is wonderful. My body and my life are gifts from God, and they are wonderful.

His works are wonderful, and I am His creation.

Let *wonderful* be our prayer when we feel insecure in who God has created us to be. Our God makes wonderful things, and we are His.

—Becca Wierwille

God, I am Your creation, and Your works are wonderful. Please give me the strength to live a full, wonderful life. Amen.

Words to Pray On

I praise you because I am fearfully and wonderfully made; your works are wonderful, I know that full well.
—Psalm 139:14 (NIV)

LORD, you are my God; I will exalt you and praise your name, for in perfect faithfulness you have done wonderful things, things planned long ago.
—Isaiah 25:1 (NIV)

Give praise to the LORD, proclaim his name; make known among the nations what he has done. Sing to him, sing praise to him; tell of all his wonderful acts. Glory in his holy name; let the hearts of those who seek the LORD rejoice. Look to the LORD and his strength; seek his face always.
—1 Chronicles 16:8–11 (NIV)

coffee

Each morning begins the same routine. The cat must be fed first or there is no peace. Then I grab the morning essentials of Bible, journal, and strong drink—coffee.

The start of the week includes words of prayer and praise in this alone time with Christ. Words flow through me onto the pages with ease. By the middle of the week, my body, mind, and spirit are not as sharp. Words don't flow anymore, but rather stumble out haphazardly onto the paper. More than one cup of coffee is needed to spark the system.

My end of the week requires stronger coffee as words congeal and refuse to participate. It is those mornings I must rely on the Holy Spirit to speak for me. The Spirit becomes that stronger cup of coffee as I trust Him to search my heart. It pleads on my behalf consistent with God's will.

—Darci Werner

Lord, I thank You for the gift of Your Spirit, who knows my inner thoughts and desires before I do, and who will intercede for me when I am exhausted and cannot put the words together.

Words to Pray On

Give strong drink to those who are perishing and
wine to those whose hearts are bitter.
—Proverbs 31:6 (CEB)

So, whether you eat or drink or whatever you do, you
should do it all for God's glory.
—1 Corinthians 10:31 (CEB)

Jesus answered, "Everyone who drinks this water will
be thirsty again, but whoever drinks from the water
that I will give will never be thirsty again. The water
that I give will become in those who drink it a spring
of water that bubbles up into eternal life."
—John 4:13–14 (CEB)

fog

Living by the water produces many foggy days. A clear walk down to the beach can quickly become a fog-filled return trip. Within minutes the familiar terrain becomes unknown and dangerous, and I cannot see what might be lurking beyond my sight line.

Fortunately, I am guided back home through the streetlights dotted along the way. Each light illuminates just a small area, but if I look and follow from one patch of light to the next, I know that I will make it safely home.

Life's troubles have a tendency to roll into our lives when we are unsuspecting. Like fog, troubles can surround and cover the clear path. Through God's Word, we receive guidance through the haze: we may only know the next step to take, but step by step, we will safely make it through.

—Virginia Ruth

God of illumination, thank You for guiding us during the foggy seasons of our lives. Through Your Word, we may walk safely home to You. Amen.

Words to Pray On

Your Word is a lamp to my feet, and a light to my path.
—Psalm 119:105 (NKJV)

However, when He, the Spirit of truth, has come,
He will guide you into all truth, for He will not speak
on his own authority, but whatever He hears He will
speak; and He will tell you things to come.
—John 16:13 (NKJV)

The humble he guides in justice, and the humble He
teaches His way. All the paths of the Lord are mercy and
truth, to such as keep His covenant and His testimonies.
—Psalm 25:9–10 (NKJV)

Whether you turn to the right or to the left, your
ears will hear a voice behind you, saying, "This is the
way; walk in it."
—Isaiah 30:21 (NIV)

choices

In the book of Ruth, three widows must move to be with family to survive in a difficult time of their lives. Orpah goes home to her family, her tribe, and their gods. Ruth decides to go with Naomi, her mother-in-law, to the land of Judah. She chooses to serve the one true God. It's a great story of God using a widow—a foreigner—in His plan. She is famous for being in the royal lineage as the grandmother of King David.

But what happened to Orpah? She's not mentioned in Scripture again, but rabbinic literature tells us she remarried and had children. One of her offspring was also famous. His name was Goliath.

Our decisions determine our destinies. What you do next matters.

—Shirley Gould

Lord, I choose to follow You. Help me make good choices that will positively affect eternity. Amen.

Words to Pray On

If serving the Lord seems undesirable to you, then
choose for yourselves this day whom you will serve....
But as for me and my household, we will serve the Lord.
—Joshua 24:15 (NIV)

But Ruth replied, "Don't urge me to leave you or to
turn back from you. Where you go I will go, and where
you stay I will stay. Your people will be my people and
your God my God. Where you die I will die, and there
I will be buried. May the Lord deal with me, be it ever
so severely, if even death separates you and me."
—Ruth 1:16–17 (NIV)

tears

"Dry up and fly right": my elementary school teacher's stern directive when I would cry from homesickness. As an adult, I still haven't dried up. When my emotions peak, tears begin to flow. I feel better, if a bit exhausted, after a good cry.

Tears are healthy. They provide the physiological release of "feel good" hormones—oxytocin and endorphins—in response to physical or emotional stress. It takes courage and strength to show our vulnerabilities through our tears.

Wait. Strength in tears? As author Charlie Mackesy wrote, "Tears fall for a reason and they are your strength, not weakness."

Jesus embraced our humanity, even our tears! The Bible records at least three times that He cried: for Jerusalem, after the death of Lazarus, and in the garden of Gethsemane.

God loves us. He sees our tears. It's OK to cry.

—Mary Bredel Fike

God, You are the source of our strength. When tears come, help me trust in Your will.

Words to Pray On

As he approached Jerusalem and saw the city, he wept over it and said, "If you, even you, had only known on this day what would bring you peace—but now it is hidden from your eyes."

—Luke 19:41–42 (NIV)

When Mary reached the place where Jesus was and saw him, she fell at his feet and said, "Lord, if you had been here, my brother would not have died." When Jesus saw her weeping, and the Jews who had come along with her also weeping, he was deeply moved in spirit and troubled. "Where have you laid him?" he asked. "Come and see, Lord," they replied. Jesus wept.

—John 11:32–35 (NIV)

During the days of Jesus' life on earth, he offered up prayers and petitions with fervent cries and tears to the one who could save him from death, and he was heard because of his reverent submission.

—Hebrews 5:7 (NIV)

walk

On the 6 millionth day of pandemic quarantine, I was starting to climb the walls. The whole family home together was amusing for the first week or so, but it quickly became overstimulating chaos, and I was losing it. So I announced I was going for a walk.

I set out with the sole intention of "walking out of myself." I needed to move, to *do* something when there was nothing I could do about all the things swirling around my head and heart…and the world at large.

In the days to come, this newfound exercise would carry me through the long days of isolation. I would just keep walking, sometimes lapping past my house several times, until I felt I had shed enough of myself to return. Even now it continues to be a useful tool for when I need to get out of my head, move my body, and walk until I return to peace.

—Sarah Greek

Help me to remember that this life is quite literally about "walking out of myself," and the destination is all of You and Your peace forever. Amen.

Words to Pray On

Follow God's example, therefore, as dearly loved children and walk in the way of love, just as Christ loved us and gave himself up for us as a fragrant offering and sacrifice to God.

—Ephesians 5:1–2 (NIV)

Blessed are those whose ways are blameless, who walk according to the law of the LORD. Blessed are those who keep his statutes and seek him with all their heart—they do not wrong but follow his ways.

—Psalm 119:1–3 (NIV)

How I long for the months gone by, for the days when God watched over me, when his lamp shone on my head and by his light I walked through darkness!

—Job 29:2–3 (NIV)

follow

Rain blurred the road as my son's windshield wipers fought a furious battle. Noah's phone had died, leaving him directionless on his stormy way home. It was then that he began to pray for help. A large dump truck pulled onto the freeway ahead of him that had the word *follow* written in yellow across the back. And that's what Noah did. He followed that truck all the way through the storm, until he recognized his way again.

Following God can often feel just as blind as my son's journey home. God promised to be a light to my path, but sometimes that path is still so hard to see. Yet, like my son, I don't have to know everything. I only have to know where God is, then simply tuck in behind His plan and follow in His steps.

—Tracy Jones

Lord, today let me follow in Your steps, no matter where You lead. I'm not safe because I have all the answers or because there isn't a storm. I am safe because You have gone before me.

Words to Pray On

To this you were called, because Christ suffered for you, leaving you an example, that you should follow in his steps.

—1 Peter 2:21 (NIV)

As Jesus was walking beside the Sea of Galilee, he saw two brothers, Simon called Peter and his brother Andrew. They were casting a net into the lake, for they were fishermen. "Come, follow me," Jesus said, "and I will send you out to fish for people." At once they left their nets and followed him. Going on from there, he saw two other brothers, James son of Zebedee and his brother John. They were in a boat with their father Zebedee, preparing their nets. Jesus called them, and immediately they left the boat and their father and followed him.

—Matthew 4:18–22 (NIV)

peace

I paddled around in the surf off Black Rock on the Hawaiian island of Maui, amazed by the myriad of fish and other sea life teeming below the surface. After 40 years of being terrified of swimming in water over my head, I never would have expected to find peace while snorkeling in the ocean. Even when a diver jumped off the cliff and landed next to me, filling my snorkel with water, a simple prayer restored my peace. Four months of fervent prayer by me and many of my friends paved the way for this miraculous peace.

Life presents frequent unexpected circumstances that agitate our calm waters and threaten the peace we find in Jesus. My first instinct in such situations is fear, but as I walk more closely with Jesus, I am learning to send up an instant prayer for peace. When I do, He is faithful to bring a peace that truly does rise above human understanding.

—Linda L. Kruschke

Heavenly Father, bring Your peace in the midst of our troubles. When storms buffet, bring Your perfect calm. Amen.

Words to Pray On

Do not be anxious about anything, but in every situation, by prayer and petition, with thanksgiving, present your requests to God. And the peace of God, which transcends all understanding, will guard your hearts and your minds in Christ Jesus.

—Philippians 4:6–7 (NIV)

The LORD sits enthroned over the flood; the LORD is enthroned as King forever. The LORD gives strength to his people; the LORD blesses his people with peace.

—Psalm 29:10–11 (NIV)

You will keep in perfect peace those whose minds are steadfast, because they trust in you. Trust in the LORD forever, for the LORD, the LORD himself, is the Rock eternal.

—Isaiah 26:3–4 (NIV)

Character cannot be developed
in ease and quiet. Only through
experience of trial and suffering
can the soul be strengthened,
ambition inspired, and
success achieved.
—Helen Keller

fireline

"Do you know what this is?" my husband asks as we hike along an overgrown forest path. I shake my head, and he tells me it is an old fireline. These man-made scars across the mountains tell stories of past wildfires. I can picture brave men and women enduring unthinkable conditions as they dug and cut these lines in the dirt and trees.

Firelines create a break in fuel, or burnable foliage, in an attempt to stop a fire in its tracks. This strategy is often a firefighter's greatest strength in the heat of the blaze. When I see these landscape scars, I'm reminded that the strength of my heart depends on God's protection. He is constantly digging firelines around my spirit and mind. Through time in His Word and prayer, I join in His work of creating a protective barrier against harmful thoughts and behaviors. He is making a safe margin around my soul.

—Eryn Lynum

Dear Lord, You are digging a fireline around my spirit. Stop any spread of harmful thoughts and attitudes. Keep me in the safety of Your presence. Amen.

Words to Pray On

Above all else, guard your heart, for everything you do flows from it.

—Proverbs 4:23 (NIV)

For he guards the course of the just and protects the way of his faithful ones. Then you will understand what is right and just and fair—every good path. For wisdom will enter your heart, and knowledge will be pleasant to your soul. Discretion will protect you, and understanding will guard you.

—Proverbs 2:8–11 (NIV)

But the Lord is faithful, and he will strengthen you and protect you from the evil one.

—2 Thessalonians 3:3 (NIV)

foreigner

When I first moved from India to the U.S. more than a decade ago, I felt like a foreigner. Almost everything in the U.S. was different, from the food to the traffic rules. The countless varieties of cereals and ice creams in supersized grocery stores amazed me. I had to learn to drive on the right side of the street since I was used to driving on the left. My brown skin and Indian accent made me stand out.

My sense of foreignness highlighted an important aspect of my biblical identity. I'm a citizen of heaven, called to live by the countercultural values of God's kingdom. Though Northern California is my home now, I will always be a foreigner on earth. I pray that my immigrant identity will always prompt me to fix my sights on my eternal home in heaven.

—Mabel Ninan

Father, teach me to hold on loosely to the things of the earth and anchor my hope and joy in You.

Words to Pray On

All these people were still living by faith when they died. They did not receive the things promised; they only saw them and welcomed them from a distance, admitting that they were foreigners and strangers on earth. People who say such things show that they are looking for a country of their own. If they had been thinking of the country they had left, they would have had opportunity to return. Instead, they were longing for a better country—a heavenly one. Therefore God is not ashamed to be called their God, for he has prepared a city for them.

—Hebrews 11:13–16 (NIV)

handcuffs

The silver handcuffs on my charm necklace remind me of novelist Elizabeth Berg's wisdom-filled words: "Don't let your habits become handcuffs."

For many years, I wrote about the shackles of chronic pain. A life sentence without mercy, I called it. Four years ago, the fiery tumor pain that had held me in bondage my whole life left. Vanished. God's mercy rewrote my life. Funny thing is, the handcuffs stuck around. Shackles in the form of words such as *Fear. If only. What if?* They'd so long been a part of me they were like old friends. Friends that let me down, dragged me down.

With God's help I replaced those handcuffs with Spirit-giving words. *Gratitude. Living in the moment. Joy.* I bid the old words farewell the way I'd once welcomed them into my mind, starting with a tiny choice that became an action, then a habit.

—Roberta Messner

Our true freedom is found in You, dear Lord.

Words to Pray On

He reached down from on high and took hold of me; he drew me out of deep waters. He rescued me from my powerful enemy, from my foes, who were too strong for me. They confronted me in the day of my disaster, but the LORD was my support. He brought me out into a spacious place; he rescued me because he delighted in me.

—Psalm 18:16–19 (NIV)

The Spirit gives life; the flesh counts for nothing. The words I have spoken to you—they are full of the Spirit and life.

—John 6:63 (NIV)

Whoever gives heed to instruction prospers, and blessed is the one who trusts in the LORD. The wise in heart are called discerning, and gracious words promote instruction.

—Proverbs 16:20–21 (NIV)

mountain

A few years ago, my family and I took a trip to Barcelona. One of the places we visited was the Sagrat Cor, a stunning church that sits atop a hill known as Mount Tibidabo.

According to Catalonian legend, Mount Tibidabo is the very mountain where the devil offered Jesus all the kingdoms of the world in exchange for His allegiance. As the Bible tells us, Jesus refused to succumb to the devil's temptation by quoting Scripture: "Away from me, Satan! For it is written: 'Worship the Lord your God, and serve him only'" (Matthew 4:10, NIV).

Of course, Mount Tibidabo is likely not the mountain where Jesus was tempted. And yet, when I stood atop its pinnacle, I was filled with awe. Jesus—a man of ordinary stature—once stood on the peak of a gigantic mountain and was—at once—greater, bigger, and infinitely more powerful. How comforting it is to know that ours is a God who understands our struggles and always stands with us on the mountains of life.

—Roma Maitlall

Jesus, whenever I feel alone, stand with me, filling me with the same courage and strength You demonstrated on the mountain.

Words to Pray On

The devil took him to a very high mountain and showed him all the kingdoms of the world and their splendor. "All this I will give you," he said, "if you will bow down and worship me."

—Matthew 4:8–9 (NIV)

So Abraham called that place The Lord Will Provide. And to this day it is said, "On the mountain of the Lord it will be provided."

—Genesis 22:14 (NIV)

His wisdom is profound, his power is vast. Who has resisted him and come out unscathed? He moves mountains without their knowing it and overturns them in his anger....He performs wonders that cannot be fathomed, miracles that cannot be counted.

—Job 9:4–5, 10 (NIV)

access

I remember when I had a single password for all my online accounts. Now—the Internet crawling with hackers and viruses and malware—we need many passwords. The strongest ones include a combination of random letters, numbers, and characters that look appropriately like a comic string of symbol cussing.

But stringent security sometimes backfires. My nephew was delayed on a return flight home recently. The problem? The IT department had secured the cockpit door from intruders so well that no one—including themselves or the pilot—could get in. My nephew watched as the ground crew literally unriveted the nose of the plane, opening it like an Easter egg so they could unlock the compartment from inside.

Our God doesn't require such extraordinary measures. Jesus's death on the cross tore down the veil that separated us from the Father, freely offering His children direct access to Him anytime, anywhere.

—Leslie McLeod

Father, what joy it gives me to know I am always welcome in Your throne room. Jesus, thank You for making a way.

Words to Pray On

Therefore, since we have been justified through faith, we have peace with God through our Lord Jesus Christ, through whom we have gained access by faith into this grace in which we now stand. And we boast in the hope of the glory of God.

—Romans 5:1–2 (NIV)

For through him we both have access to the Father by one Spirit. Consequently, you are no longer foreigners and strangers, but fellow citizens with God's people and also members of his household, built on the foundations of the apostles and prophets, with Christ Jesus himself as the chief cornerstone.

—Ephesians 2:18–20 (NIV)

Open for me the gates of the righteous; I will enter and give thanks to the LORD. This is the gate of the LORD through which the righteous may enter. I will give you thanks, for you answered me; you have become my salvation.

—Psalm 118:19–21 (NIV)

handrails

A few years ago, I visited Abraham Lincoln's home in Springfield, Illinois. I tried to imagine Mr. and Mrs. Lincoln in those rooms. I felt their presence most strongly when the docent said a curious thing as we were heading upstairs. She said to hold on to the handrail and pointed out that it was the same handrail Mr. Lincoln's hands would have touched. So we could think of it as though we were "shaking hands" with Abe Lincoln!

Dictionaries describe a handrail as a support or guard on a stairway or platform. Metaphorically, I've had people in my life who were "handrails." My husband is one. I recently broke my right foot, and he had to drive me everywhere I needed to go.

"Handrails" connect us to others, guide us, and protect us. And by grasping them, we "shake hands" with all those who came before and will come after.

—Nancy Schrock

Lord, thank You for the many handrails You've given me in my life. May I provide strength as a handrail to others.

Words to Pray On

If anyone serves, they should do so with the strength
God provides, so that in all things God may be
praised through Jesus Christ.

—1 Peter 4:11 (NIV)

They confronted me in the day of my disaster, but the
Lord was my support. He brought me out into a spacious
place; he rescued me because he delighted in me.

—2 Samuel 22:19–20 (NIV)

When he hesitated, the men grasped his hand and the
hands of his wife and of his two daughters and led
them safely out of the city, for the Lord was merciful
to them.

—Genesis 19:16 (NIV)

counsel

Being a single mom is not the plan I envisioned for my life, but this is the path I have walked with the Lord, and He has been faithful. When life became hard, God provided the amazing gift of godly counselors.

One night, the pain of being abandoned was so much that I couldn't catch my breath. My chest hurt and darkness enveloped me. All I could do was cry out, "Jesus!" He met me there, and He was my next breath and my next. Over the following days and months, He soothed my heart with wisdom from His Word, led me to amazing pastors, and guided me to healing through godly counselors. All these people pointed me back to the most incredible counselor ever: the One who is with us forever, the One who helps us breathe, heal, and even find joy again.

—Amy Wallace

Lord, counsel me and lead me in the path that brings You glory. Amen.

Words to Pray On

And I will ask the Father, and He will give you another Counselor to be with you forever.

—John 14:16 (HCSB)

Wisdom and strength belong to God; counsel and understanding are His.

—Job 12:13 (HCSB)

I will praise the LORD who counsels me—even at night my conscience instructs me. I keep the LORD in mind always. Because He is at my right hand, I will not be shaken.

—Psalm 16:7–8 (HCSB)

Listen to counsel and receive instruction so that you may be wise later in life.

—Proverbs 19:20 (HCSB)

climb

With nothing but an uncharted Saturday ahead, my husband and I set out on a 7-mile, out-and-back hike. The trail was steep, hot, and poorly marked. I soon sported an array of cuts and scrapes from scrambling over rocks.

"What is this trail called?" I asked, really meaning: *Why did you bring me out here to die?*

"The Midlife Crisis Trail," my husband answered.

His grin told me he'd waited all afternoon to say it. I giggled. Of course Midlife Crisis would be hot, poorly marked, and rocky.

But you know what else Midlife Crisis offered? Sweeping city views. We could see for miles.

So many of us have questions about the twists and turns of our lives. Sometimes God gives us perspective on how far we've climbed and how much we've endured. That's a good spot to thank Him for walking with us—especially when the trail was poorly marked.

—Laurie Davies

Lord, when the trail is hard and we don't feel like climbing anymore, please remind us that You are the one who directs our paths. Amen.

Words to Pray On

Brothers and sisters, I do not consider myself yet to have taken hold of it. But one thing I do: Forgetting what is behind and straining toward what is ahead, I press on toward the goal to win the prize for which God has called me heavenward in Christ Jesus.

—Philippians 3:13–14 (NIV)

My steps have held to your paths; my feet have not stumbled.

—Psalm 17:5 (NIV)

Who may ascend the mountain of the Lord? Who may stand in his holy place? The one who has clean hands and a pure heart, who does not trust in an idol or swear by a false god.

—Psalm 24:3–4 (NIV)

And the God of all grace, who called you to his eternal glory in Christ, after you have suffered a little while, will himself restore you and make you strong, firm and steadfast.

—1 Peter 5:10 (NIV)

spinach

My favorite color? Green. My favorite vegetable? Spinach. Is it surprising, then, that a favorite cartoon of mine starred Popeye the Sailor Man? Why Popeye? His extraordinary strength stemmed from his consuming spinach, a green vegetable he poured directly from the can into his mouth.

The Popeye cartoon theme song I sang as a child includes the lyrics, "I'm strong to the 'finich' 'cause I eats my spinach." But the strength spinach provided eventually dissipated. Popeye searched for cans of the iron-rich veggie when the next need for superstrength arose.

Like Popeye, Christians can access incredible strength. Our weakness offers the opportunity, and usually spurs us to seek, the amazing and divine power available to us through our Savior. A simple prayer for help, though—not a canned vegetable— allows us to overcome our lack of strength.

—Alice H. Murray

Dear God, I acknowledge my weakness. Thank You for providing me with access to the astounding strength offered to me by Jesus, who is for Christians what spinach is for Popeye. Amen.

Words to Pray On

For when I am weak, then I am strong.
—2 Corinthians 12:10 (NIV)

He gives strength to the weary and increases the power of the weak. Even youths grow tired and weary, and young men stumble and fall; but those who hope in the Lord will renew their strength. They will soar on wings like eagles; they will run and not grow weary, they will walk and not be faint.
—Isaiah 40:29–31 (NIV)

The Lord is my strength and my defense; he has become my salvation. He is my God, and I will praise him, my father's God, and I will exalt him.
—Exodus 15:2 (NIV)

pieces

Every time my dad returned from a business trip, he brought me a fragile porcelain teacup. He chose their patterns thoughtfully: gentle green vines and delicate pink buds, a kitten with a ball of yarn, swallows circling the rim. Each one unique and perfect.

One day, I toppled the shelf where I kept all of my dad's gifts, and they shattered on the floor. I sank beside them weeping, their lovely designs now a mess of broken pieces. In a single moment of carelessness, I destroyed the beautiful gifts I'd loved.

My older brother stood over me shaking his head. "You worry too much. Dad will understand, and it will all be OK." The next morning, I awoke to find every precious little treasure mended and back where it belonged. There were no scars from the fall or pieces missing. My brother made sure of it, and my dad never stopped giving me fragile gifts.

—Kimberly Shumate

Jesus, thank You for mending my shattered pieces and returning me to a position of wholeness and strength. Amen.

Words to Pray On

He who was seated on the throne said, "I am making everything new!"

—Revelation 21:5 (NIV)

The steadfast love of the Lord never ceases; his mercies never come to an end; they are new every morning.

—Lamentations 3:22–23 (ESV)

And a man with a shriveled hand was there. Then [Jesus] said to the man, "Stretch out your hand." So he stretched it out and it was completely restored, just as sound as the other.

—Matthew 12:10, 13 (NIV)

God, pick up the pieces. Put me back together again. You are my praise!

—Jeremiah 17:14 (MSG)

song

I had been through a very difficult time. On this particular morning, I thought of a story about an African village told to me by a close friend. In the village, when a person experienced a tragedy or was in mourning, they would be sent away for 30 days to sing out their sadness. My friend had suggested that I do a similar thing.

I decided to sing my morning prayers. At first it seemed awkward, but almost immediately I could feel the burdens in my mind being lifted. The more I sang, the lighter I felt, and the more present God became to me. Soon I grew strong enough to face another day with joy in my heart. Singing a song is a healing way to pray.

—Linda Marie

Dear Lord, please place a song—and a steadfast trust in Your love—in my heart.

Words to Pray On

See, God has come to save me! I will trust and not
be afraid, for the Lord is my strength and song; he is
my salvation. Oh, the joy of drinking deeply from the
Fountain of Salvation!

—Isaiah 12:2–3 (TLB)

All your waves and billows have gone over me, and
floods of sorrow pour upon me like a thundering
cataract. Yet day by day the LORD also pours out his
steadfast love upon me, and through the night I sing
his songs and pray to God who gives me life.

—Psalm 42:7–8 (TLB)

Talk with each other about the Lord, quoting psalms
and hymns and singing sacred songs, making music in
your hearts to the Lord.

—Ephesians 5:19 (TLB)

signs

Sometimes I wonder: *Does God see me? Does He hear me? Is He even there?* That's when I know it's time to get outside and look for signs in nature.

When I take my dog, Scarlett, for a walk at the park, I see two baby squirrels with tiny tails chasing each other across our path. When we arrive in the woods, I hear the chorus of frogs joining with the new songs of the birds to greet us. God's handiwork is strewn throughout the forest in broad strokes of green woven throughout the woods.

Surrounded by the vastness of his creation, I feel small but seen. My heart and my eyes open to the signs He is showing me, shoring up my faith and reminding me He is all around.

—Amy Catlin Wozniak

Dear Lord, thank You for reminding me that to see You I need only to walk in Your creation, where signs of You are all around. Amen.

Words to Pray On

The heavens proclaim the glory of God. The skies display his craftsmanship. Day after day they continue to speak; night after night they make him known.
—Psalm 19:1–2 (NLT)

How great are his signs, how powerful his wonders! His kingdom will last forever, his rule through all generations.
—Daniel 4:3 (NLT)

So I have reason to be enthusiastic about all Christ Jesus has done through me in my service to God. Yet I dare not boast about anything except what Christ has done through me, bringing the Gentiles to God by my message and by the way I worked among them. They were convinced by the power of miraculous signs and wonders and by the power of God's Spirit.
—Romans 15:17–19 (NLT)

share

I debated. Then I tapped out the text. "This is hard for me to do," I wrote. "But I'm asking for your prayers."

Still somewhat hesitant, I told my neighbor Marcella about my eye condition and the eyestrain it caused. How I'd been trying to trust God to heal me, but that I complained a lot to my husband. Could she please pray that God would take away the floaters in my eyes and give me patience in the meantime?

"You are on our church prayer list," she typed back. "You will be prayed for by many."

A few hours later, my eyestrain lifted. Lesson learned: Don't ever be afraid to share your burdens.

—Sheryl Smith-Rodgers

Thank You, Jesus, for giving me the courage to share my troubles with others, and for the believers who lift us up when we do.

Words to Pray On

Share each other's burdens, and in this way obey the
law of Christ.

—Galatians 6:2 (NLT)

When three of Job's friends heard of the tragedy he
had suffered, they got together and traveled from
their homes to comfort and console him.

—Job 2:11 (NLT)

Share your food with the hungry, and give shelter to the
homeless. Give clothes to those who need them, and
do not hide from relatives who need your help. Then
your salvation will come like the dawn, and your wounds
will quickly heal. Your godliness will lead you forward,
and the glory of the Lord will protect you from behind.

—Isaiah 58:7–8 (NLT)

treasure

In most treasure hunt movies, it seems the characters always end up stumbling around in a dark cave following a map. When they finally round the last corner, and the light from their torches reaches the innermost space, they discover stacks of diamonds, rubies, and gold. Had they turned back too early, or if their lights had not reached quite that far, they would have missed those riches of untold measure.

When God created me in the dark cave of my mother's womb, He tucked gifts and talents within me. If I only look outward, living according to the world's definition of success, all He's given me remains in the dark, undiscovered. When I embrace God's definition of success, His grace extends deep within, illuminating my true gifts and talents. If I then use them to build His kingdom here on earth, I'll become a treasure of untold measure to others.

—Claire McGarry

Wondrous God, thank You for the gifts and talent You've bestowed upon me. May I use them to glorify You. Amen.

Words to Pray On

For you created my inmost being; you knit me together in my mother's womb. I praise you because I am fearfully and wonderfully made.

—Psalm 139:13–14 (NIV)

Out of all the peoples on the face of the earth, the LORD has chosen you to be his treasured possession.

—Deuteronomy 14:2 (NIV)

But he knows the way that I take; when he has tested me, I will come forth as gold. My feet have closely followed his steps; I have kept to his way without turning aside. I have not departed from the commands of his lips; I have treasured the words of his mouth more than my daily bread.

—Job 23:10–12 (NIV)

The God we serve does not seek
out the perfect, but instead uses our
imperfections and our shortcomings
for His greater good. I am humbled
by my own limitations. But where
I am weak, He is strong.
—Rick Perry

wait

When my husband and I were in the market for our first house, we prayed, asking God to lead us all along the way. We worked with a real estate agent, created our wish list of desired features and area of town, and secured financing, both with a bank loan and a gift from a relative for the down payment. But after we found a great house in a wonderful neighborhood, it turned out that there was a misunderstanding about the gift from our relative, and that financial help wasn't going to come through. Without that help, we couldn't afford this house. We were so disappointed!

And so we waited, confident that God would bring something better. After many more months of waiting, we were able to build a new house in a brand-new community. This allowed us to customize features and build friendships literally from the ground up. If we can be patient and wait on God, His provision is always better.

—Stephanie Reeves

Dear Lord, You are Jehovah Jireh, the God who supplies. We don't always know when, and we don't always know why You say no to certain things we've asked for, but You always provide for our needs. Amen.

Words to Pray On

Wait for the Lᴏʀᴅ; be strong, and let your heart take courage; wait for the Lᴏʀᴅ!

—Psalm 27:14 (ESV)

Our soul waits for the Lᴏʀᴅ; he is our help and our shield.

—Psalm 33:20 (ESV)

But for you, O Lᴏʀᴅ, do I wait; it is you, O Lord my God, who will answer.

—Psalm 38:15 (ESV)

Be like men who are waiting for their master to come home from the wedding feast, so that they may open the door to him at once when he comes and knocks.

—Luke 12:36 (ESV)

bold

My friend Liz asked our mutual friend Wayne to sing at her mother's funeral. When Wayne in turn asked me to accompany him on the piano, I wanted to say no. I don't play well. Years had passed since I'd played in front of anyone. Saying yes seemed like a bold, audacious move. But the funeral was in another town and only a handful of us could attend. How could I refuse?

"God, I'm scared. Help me," became my prayer all the way to the church, where a beautiful grand piano designed for more deserving talent stood waiting. Thankfully, Wayne's solo was early in the program, so I didn't have long to quake. His strong voice covered my inadequacies and we conquered. Afterward, I felt so thankful I hadn't allowed fear to rob me of the chance to honor my friend in this way.

—Terrie Todd

Father, grant me boldness to step through doors of opportunity that You open before me so I can bless others. Amen.

Words to Pray On

When I called, you answered me; you greatly embold-
ened me.

—Psalm 138:3 (NIV)

The wicked flee though no one pursues, but the righteous are as bold as a lion.

—Proverbs 28:1 (NIV)

Pray also for me, that whenever I speak, words may be
given me so that I will fearlessly make known the mys-
tery of the gospel, for which I am an ambassador in
chains. Pray that I may declare it fearlessly, as I should.

—Ephesians 6:19–20 (NIV)

generous

A friend of mine constantly surprises me with her generosity. She doesn't limit her affection to presenting others with spontaneous gifts. When I need a confidante to walk with me and talk me through a situation, she's there to listen and offer support.
If she sees me struggling with an assignment for work, she often offers a solution before I even realize there is a problem. It's as if she lives in a state of perpetual kindness, blessing others wherever she sees fit.

Her generous heart encourages me to seek to fill the needs of others just as she does. It's not a natural part of my personality, but it's becoming more automatic the more often I do it.

Whenever I think of her, I smile. I think God does too.

—Heidi Gaul

God, help me see the needs of others and fill them. Let me be Your generous hands. Amen.

Words to Pray On

But a generous man devises generous things, and by generosity he shall stand.

—Isaiah 32:8 (NKJV)

The generous soul will be made rich, and he who waters will also be watered himself.

—Proverbs 11:25 (NKJV)

He who has a generous eye will be blessed, for he gives of his bread to the poor.

—Proverbs 22:9 (NKJV)

Give generously to them and do so without a grudging heart; then because of this the LORD your God will bless you in all your work and in everything you put your hand to.

—Deuteronomy 15:10 (NIV)

create

I worked with hospitalized children for many years as a child life specialist. My job involved incorporating play and creative expression as a means of helping children cope with the pain and stress they often experienced. At bedsides and in playrooms, I witnessed how powerfully play and creativity engage our imagination and spark our soul. Children leave play experiences more peaceful and fulfilled than they were before, and I believe that is evidence of how our souls prosper in the process.

In the Bible, we are first introduced to God as a creative being, and we are told that we are made in God's image. Just imagine the power God released and the thoughts He had as He brought the world into being. And in response, His creation worshipped Him!

May we use the blessings of our creative nature and imagination in our everyday lives to praise the One who first made us.

—Shannon Alford

Lord, all things are created through You and by You. Bless the work of my hands to glorify You. Amen.

Words to Pray On

In the beginning God created the heavens and the earth.

—Genesis 1:1 (NIV)

All creatures look to you to give them their food at the proper time....When you send your Spirit, they are created, and you renew the face of the ground.

—Psalm 104:27, 30 (NIV)

For in him all things are created: things in heaven and on earth, visible and invisible, whether thrones or powers or rulers or authorities; all things have been created through him and for him. He is before all things, and in him all things hold together.

—Colossians 1:16–17 (NIV)

footprints

I know the birds have been at my feeder. Not because I heard their chirps, or the flutter of their wings past my window. But I see their footprints, a circuitous path of tiny pitchforks as they search for fallen sunflower seeds.

The footprints are evident in spring, left behind on soppy mud. And they're obvious in winter, on fresh white snow. But in summer when the grass is tall, or fall when the ground is thick with leaves, there are no footprints to be found.

Just because I see no footprints, it doesn't mean that the birds were absent that day. They were there, hopping and pecking as usual. It's the same way with God. Sometimes I clearly see His footprints as he lays out His plan for me, and sometimes his footprints are vague and hidden. But I can trust that he is always there, making mighty paths.

—Peggy Frezon

Lord, I sometimes grow discouraged when I don't see evidence of Your presence. Please make my faith stronger than my need for proof.

Words to Pray On

Your path led through the sea, your way through the mighty waters, though your footprints were not seen.
                              —Psalm 77:19 (NIV)

Has any god ever tried to take for himself one nation out of another nation, by testings, by signs and wonders, by war, by a mighty hand and an outstretched arm, or by great and awesome deeds, like all the things the Lord your God did for you in Egypt before your very eyes?
                              —Deuteronomy 4:34 (NIV)

Then Moses said, "Now show me your glory." And the Lord said, "I will cause all my goodness to pass in front of you, and I will proclaim my name, the Lord, in your presence. I will have mercy on whom I will have mercy, and I will have compassion on whom I will have compassion. But," he said, "you cannot see my face, for no one may see me and live."
                              —Exodus 33:18–20 (NIV)

pool

Central air conditioning and swimming pools were considered luxuries in my childhood. In the searing heat of a Florida summer, I cherished the few times I was invited out of the dry, hot wilderness and into a friend's swimming pool to jump and splash with abandon. Nothing ever felt so refreshing!

As a young wife, I found refreshment through spontaneous potluck suppers, when couples pooled their meager casseroles to create a feast—something none of us could have provided on our own. During hard times, when my own prayer life would falter, friends would pool their faith and their prayers to help gently guide me out of the dry land of doubt. When I felt confused or despondent about my mothering skills, I could find help in the pool of wisdom that other mothers offered.

Pools come in many forms, but they always provide the refreshment we need.

—Mary Hix

Renewing One, show me how to be a pool of refreshment to those who need that today. Amen.

Words to Pray On

He turns a wilderness into a pool of water and a dry land into springs of water; and He has the hungry live there, so that they may establish an inhabited city, and sow fields and plant vineyards, and gather a fruitful harvest.

—Psalm 107:35–37 (NASB)

Then those who limp will leap like a deer, and the tongue of those who cannot speak will shout for joy. For waters will burst forth in the wilderness, and streams in the desert. The scorched land will become a pool and the thirst ground springs of water; in the haunt of jackals, its resting place, grass becomes reeds and rushes. A highway will be there, a roadway, and it will be called the Highway of Holiness.

—Isaiah 35:6–8 (NASB)

tenacity

Driving to the gym one day, I heard a story on the radio that really hit a nerve. A nurse had interviewed dozens of terminally ill patients in hospice care and asked them about their deepest regrets. The most frequent response she received was, "I wish I'd had the tenacity to live a life true to myself, not the life others expected of me."

Her observation forced me to examine my life and define what tenacity looked like for me. I have chased recognition all my life—the classic people pleaser. I prayed and made a commitment to transform myself from a people-pleaser to a God-pleaser.

I see tenacity as a mixture of resolve, strength, courage, endurance, and hope. It took resolve to go against my natural instinct to seek acceptance and approval and firmly stand on God's Word; strength not to fall back into a "what will they think of me" frame of mind; courage to turn my back on consumerism; endurance to set healthy boundaries; and hope that I could discard my cover girl mask. In God's perfect time, I reaped a harvest of blessing.

—Kimberly Davidson

Lord, I pray You give me the strength and tenacity to live a focused and enthusiastic life for You today. Amen.

Words to Pray On

So, my dear brothers and sisters, be strong and immovable. Always work enthusiastically for the Lord, for you know that nothing you do for the Lord is ever useless.
—1 Corinthians 15:58 (NLT)

But those who live to please the Spirit will harvest everlasting life from the Spirit. So let's not get tired of doing what is good. At just the right time we will reap a harvest of blessing if we don't give up. Therefore, whenever we have the opportunity, we should do good to everyone—especially to those in the family of faith.
—Galatians 6:8–10 (NLT)

This is my command—be strong and courageous! Do not be afraid or discouraged. For the LORD your God is with you wherever you go.
—Joshua 1:9 (NLT)

meek

Heat rose in my face as I reread the email. It wasn't the response I'd expected. I'd reached out for help, but my supervisor had heaped more onto my overflowing workload. And this wasn't the first time. I typed a hasty response. My finger hovered over the Send button.

But instead of sending it, I paused and let a word echo through my mind and into my heart. *Meek.* Jesus said the meek will inherit the earth, but what does it mean to be meek?

Meekness is gentleness and patience. It's choosing peace when someone steps on your toes. It's submitting to your boss, even when reading her email makes you cringe.

To be meek is to be like Jesus. Gentle with broken people. Patient with a hurting world. Ready to love and not attack, even when one of those feels much easier than the other.

—Becca Wierwille

God, transform my heart so I can be meek and live in a way that defies the world's standards. Amen.

Words to Pray On

Blessed are the meek, for they will inherit the earth.
—Matthew 5:5 (NIV)

But I will leave within you the meek and humble.
The remnant of Israel will trust in the name of the Lord.
They will do no wrong; they will tell no lies. A deceitful tongue will not be found in their mouths. They will eat and lie down and no one will make them afraid.
—Zephaniah 3:12–13 (NIV)

Refrain from anger and turn from wrath; do not fret—it leads only to evil. For those who are evil will be destroyed, but those who hope in the Lord will inherit the land. A little while, and the wicked will be no more; though you look for them, they will not be found. But the meek will inherit the land and enjoy peace and prosperity.
—Psalm 37:8–11 (NIV)

with

A friend of mine needed help with childcare, and I happily volunteered. Her daughter didn't know me yet, and when my friend arrived, the daughter hid behind her mother's legs. My friend pried tiny fingers from her skirt, bent down to eye level, and asked her daughter, "What will you remember today?"

I watched, wondering how this little girl would answer. I thought she might say: *I'll be a good listener,* or *I'll eat all my lunch.* Instead, with her bottom lip quivering, she said, "I'll remember that Jesus is with me."

Believing that Jesus is with us gives courage in the midst of uncertainty. He's with us when we receive hard news. He's with us when we feel misunderstood. He's with us when we suffer painful circumstances. No matter what we face today, Jesus is with us.

—Kate Rietema

Dear Jesus, I believe You are always with me. Amen.

Words to Pray On

And surely I am with you always, to the very end of
the age.

—Matthew 28:20 (NIV)

That night the Lord appeared to him and said, "I am
the God of your father Abraham. Do not be afraid, for
I am with you."

—Genesis 26:24 (NIV)

We wait in hope for the Lord; he is our help and our
shield. In him our hearts rejoice, for we trust in his
holy name. May your unfailing love be with us, Lord,
even as we put our hope in you.

—Psalm 33:20–22 (NIV)

relentless

Something continued to gnaw at me when I woke after a long restless night of sleep. It bothered me throughout the day, picking at my soul and pestering my thoughts.

Our son suffered from decisions that had forced him out of our home and into a heartless world. I wanted him to know we loved him despite everything and that God would find him.

When I settled to pray, the word *relentless* dug deep. God relentlessly reminded me that He was omnipresent and watched over the things we could not control. I cried out, *Father, love our son with Your deep, relentless love. Pursue him like the shepherd searching until he finds the lost sheep. Bring him home. Relentlessly love him.*

—Cindy K. Sproles

Lord God, love us with Your relentless love. Please don't stop.

Words to Pray On

If a man has a hundred sheep and one of them gets lost, what will he do? Won't he leave the ninety-nine others in the wilderness and go to search for the one that is lost until he finds it?

—Luke 15:4 (NLT)

They will be my people, and I will be their God. And I will give them one heart and one purpose: to worship me forever, for their own good and for the good of all their descendants. And I will make an everlasting covenant with them: I will never stop doing good for them. I will put a desire in their hearts to worship me, and they will never leave me. I will find joy doing good for them and will faithfully and wholeheartedly replant them in this land.

—Jeremiah 32:38–41 (NLT)

courage

When I was in seventh grade, I was the second to the last junior-high student to jump off the top of a 2-story boat into the water.

It was a vacation day at my boarding school, and the students from my dorm were picnicking on a small island near the school. Our dorm parent challenged all the junior high kids to either dive or jump off the top deck of the boat—and his "challenge" was more of a mandate. Frightened or not, I had to go.

That was 46 years ago, and I can still remember the terror of falling from that height and the shame I felt about not having the courage to jump sooner.

It takes fear to have courage. Why? As pastor R. C. Sproul observes, it doesn't take courage to do something you are not afraid to do.

Moses encourages us to "be strong" and "take courage" in the decisions we make, knowing God is right beside us, and that He will never leave us.

Having courage is a decision we make, sometimes moment by moment, when things are going tough.

—Sharon J. Morris

Dear Heavenly Father, thank You for giving us courage in the face of our fears. Amen.

Words to Pray On

Be strong. Take courage. Don't be intimidated. Don't
give them a second thought because God, your God,
is striding ahead of you. He's right there with you. He
won't let you down; he won't leave you.
—Deuteronomy 31:6 (MSG)

God is a safe place to hide, ready to help when
we need him. We stand fearless at the cliff-edge
of doom, courageous in seastorm and earthquake,
before the rush and roar of oceans, the tremors that
shift mountains. Jacob-wrestling God fights for us,
God-of-Angel-Armies protects us.
—Psalm 46:1–3 (MSG)

cover

I leave my birthday cards on display for a month or more after my birthday. I love cards, not just birthday but Christmas, Easter, anniversary. I love them all, but that's not the only reason I leave them out so long. I use them as a reminder to pray. Each morning I pick a different card and pray for the person who sent the card to me. I ask God to extend His hand and cover the sender. To grant them good health and protection. To fulfill their every need. Sometimes I pray just one word—*cover.*

I make and send out a lot of cards too. Just before I drop each card through the mail slot, I pray for the recipient: "Cover them, Lord."

—Pamela Haskin

When things are difficult for me, Lord, extend Your hand and cover me, too, with Your love and grace.

Words to Pray On

I pray that you may enjoy good health and that all
may go well with you.

—3 John 2 (NIV)

He will cover you with his feathers, and under his
wings you will find refuge; his faithfulness will be your
shield and rampart.

—Psalm 91:4 (NIV)

Blessed are those whose transgressions are forgiven,
whose sins are covered. Blessed is the one whose sin
the Lord will never count against them.

—Romans 4:7–8 (NIV)

heavy

When I was growing up, I had a shelf that was basically a board attached to brackets so it looked like it was floating on the wall. Well, I have to admit that my room wasn't always the tidiest. Each day that shelf gathered more and more little things: books, stuffed animals, framed pictures, coins from my pocket, etc. I did not realize how heavy a lot of little things could end up being until one day, out of the blue—CRASH! The shelf gave out and all of the little items fell to the floor in one big mess.

Sometimes I have to remind myself to lay every burden before God and stop trying to carry all the little everyday worries that add up to a heavy weight. He sees the heaviness as it grows and grows, and if we ask, He will replace it with His burden—which is light because Jesus already carried it.

—Juliette Alvey

Lord, things are becoming too heavy for me. Please lift these burdens and give me rest. Amen.

Words to Pray On

Come to me, all you who are weary and burdened, and I will give you rest. Take my yoke upon you and learn from me, for I am gentle and humble in heart, and you will find rest for your souls. For my yoke is easy and my burden is light.

—Matthew 11:28–30 (NIV)

Praise be to the Lord, to God our Savior, who daily bears our burdens. Our God is a God who saves; from the Sovereign LORD comes escape from death.

—Psalm 68:19–20 (NIV)

What you are doing is not good. You and these people who come to you will only wear yourselves out. The work is too heavy for you; you cannot handle it alone. Listen now to me and I will give you some advice, and may God be with you....

—Exodus 18:17–19 (NIV)

silence

The morning sun begins to filter through the living room windows as I sit to relax in my favorite chair with my fingers wrapped around a cup of hot tea. A time for silence, peace, and reflection. I savor this quiet time to plan and pray before the "daily busyness" begins.

How do you feel about spending time in silence? Silence stimulates our brain to process our thoughts and relieve tension. Removed from the cacophony of today's high-tech sensory overload, we can find inner strength and peace. We can choose to slow down and enjoy the beauty of our world.

The four Gospels describe Jesus retreating to quiet places, where He found solitude to pray and listen to His Father. In the silence, He found strength to carry out His ministry.

It was in the "gentle whisper" that Elijah heard God's call. In our silence, we can hear God too.

—Mary Bredel Fike

Lord, help me to embrace silence in my daily routine to listen prayerfully to You and Your plan for my life.

Words to Pray On

He says, "Be still, and know that I am God; I will be exalted among the nations, I will be exalted in the earth."

—Psalm 46:10 (NIV)

The LORD said, "Go out and stand on the mountain in the presence of the LORD, for the LORD is about to pass by." Then a great and powerful wind tore the mountains apart and shattered the rocks before the LORD, but the LORD was not in the wind. After the wind there was an earthquake, but the LORD was not in the earthquake. After the earthquake came a fire, but the LORD was not in the fire. And after the fire came a gentle whisper.

—1 Kings 19:11–12 (NIV)

After he had dismissed them, he went up on a mountainside by himself to pray.

—Matthew 14:23 (NIV)

Don't wish me happiness…Wish
me courage and strength and a sense
of humor—I will need them all.
—Anne Morrow Lindbergh

reward

A little girl I nannied struggled with reading. She couldn't read the content for her grade level, and the easier material was too boring for her to invest the effort for an uninspiring return. We practiced sight words—words that young children should be able to identify without sounding them out—and wrestled through phonics books she hated until I got an idea.

We picked some chapter books with great stories. She had to read the first page of each chapter (with much encouragement and assistance), then I would read the rest of that chapter to her. It took some convincing. There were longer sentences and hard words she couldn't pronounce. One page could seem impossible at first glance. But after a few chapters, she was snatching the book back from me. She attacked her challenge so she could find out what happened next! The return on her investment finally exceeded her struggle.

—Sarah Greek

Thank you, God, for honoring our daily struggles. When we give our best, You meet us with a bigger return to inspire us in our hard work.

Words to Pray On

The desires of the diligent are fully satisfied.

—Proverbs 13:4 (NIV)

This is what the LORD says: "Restrain your voice from weeping and your eyes from tears, for your work will be rewarded."

—Jeremiah 31:16 (NIV)

So do not throw away your confidence; it will be richly rewarded. You need to persevere so that when you have done the will of God, you will receive what he has promised.

—Hebrews 10:35–36 (NIV)

marvelous

As I watched the bridal dance, one word came to mind: *marvelous*. The couple had met through mutual friends. Like-minded in faith and ministry, they fell in love and were a match made in heaven.

Excellent, splendid, glorious. Yes, marvelous.

We've all seen marvelous sights: a sweet newborn baby, a breathtaking landscape, a magnificent sunset. As beautiful as those are, *marvelous* also happens when God equips us for a task that surprises us. Perhaps we know *marvelous* when we draw on His courage to move in obedience, or to move with grace for challenging relationships.

Where in your observations or personal experience have you met *marvelous*? Let's remember to thank Him for His marvelous works in our lives.

—Marilyn Nutter

Father, forgive me for not remembering that even my breath is marvelous because it is Your work. Thank You for the marvelous works You have done. Amen.

Words to Pray On

Remember His marvelous works which He has done,
His wonders, and the judgments of His mouth.

—1 Chronicles 16:12 (NKJV)

But as for me, I would seek God, and to God I would
commit my cause—who does great things, and
unsearchable, marvelous things without number.
He gives rain on the earth, and sends waters on the
fields. He sets on high those who are lowly, and those
who mourn are lifted to safety. . . . So the poor have
hope, and injustice shuts her mouth.

—Job 5:8–11, 16 (NKJV)

The stone which the builders rejected has become
the chief cornerstone. This was the LORD's doing, and
it is marvelous in our eyes.

—Matthew 21:42 (NKJV)

carry

The decision to move was exciting. The implementation, not so much. After a few weeks of carrying a box or two each day up to our second-floor apartment, I was done, physically and emotionally. *Will this job ever be finished?*

At just the right moment, my brother-in-law volunteered his truck. His family helped carry the truckload of boxes to the truck and up the stairs at the other end. Forming an assembly line, each person only took a few steps before handing boxes to the next person. A short while later, the last box entered the apartment. The dreaded job was done without anyone being worn out. We sat on the couches, relaxing the rest of the day.

It reminded me of my mom saying, "Many hands make light work." Never have those words been so obvious in my life as that Saturday.

—Beth Gormong

Lord, thank You for Your strong arms and for helping me when my load becomes heavy. Help me see when others need my help. Amen.

Words to Pray On

Carry each other's burdens, and in this way you will fulfill the law of Christ.

—Galatians 6:2 (NIV)

The Lᴏʀᴅ is the strength of his people, a fortress of salvation for his anointed one. Save your people and bless your inheritance; be their shepherd and carry them forever.

—Psalm 28:8–9 (NIV)

Listen to me, you descendants of Jacob, all the remnant of the people of Israel, you whom I have upheld since your birth, and have carried since you were born. Even to your old age and gray hairs I am he, I am he who will sustain you. I have made you and I will carry you; I will sustain you and I will rescue you.

—Isaiah 46:3–4 (NIV)

daily

When I accepted the challenge of running the 2021 New York City Marathon with Team World Vision, I was both excited and apprehensive. Running the iconic NYC marathon would be thrilling, but could I endure the 20 weeks of training? The journey to the finish line—26.2 miles and 20 children sponsored through World Vision—seemed overwhelming.

But my outlook changed when I focused on praying daily for my daily needs. As Jesus taught His disciples (and us!) to pray.

On days when I felt worn out or discouraged: *Lord, please give me the strength and energy I need—today!* On days when running felt easier: *Thank You, God!* I discovered that when I relied on Him daily, He gave me what I needed daily.

At the end of 20 weeks, with the Lord's daily provision, I made it across the finish line!

—Lisa Lenning

Lord, I ask for Your daily provision, for today. You are the Giver of all I need. Amen.

Words to Pray On

Give us this day our daily bread.

—Matthew 6:11 (ESV)

Blessed be the Lord, who daily bears us up; God is our salvation.

—Psalm 68:19 (ESV)

And now, O sons, listen to me: blessed are those who keep my ways. Hear instruction and be wise, and do not neglect it. Blessed is the one who listens to me, watching daily at my gates, waiting beside my doors.

—Proverbs 8:32–34 (ESV)

My feet have closely followed his steps; I have kept to his way without turning aside. I have not departed from the commands of his lips; I have treasured the words of his mouth more than my daily bread.

—Job 23:11–12 (NIV)

anchor

We let down the anchor from our canoe. The lake bed is hard, composed of rocks compressed over a vast amount of time. The anchor holds strong, keeping us steady on the water's surface. My husband and I watch our sons paddling their kayak nearby.

My thoughts reflect off the water, carrying memories from my childhood on another lake far from here. That lake, home to so many of my childhood summers in the Midwest, has a soft, mucky bottom. We have a longstanding family joke about how many anchors we lost to the mud's suction. My father would pull in the anchor line only to find it empty-ended, another anchor swallowed by the earth.

I learned from a young age that it matters what I anchor to. If anchored to soft, penetrable ground, my faith risks being engulfed by the world's arguments or my own doubts. But if I anchor my beliefs on the rock-solid foundation of God's Word, I cannot be moved.

—Eryn Lynum

Dear Lord, my hope is anchored in Your steadfast love. Your salvation is my strong foundation. Amen.

Words to Pray On

We have this hope as an anchor for the soul, firm and secure.

—Hebrews 6:19 (NIV)

Therefore this is what the Lord God says: "Behold, I am laying a stone in Zion, a tested stone, a precious cornerstone for the foundation, firmly placed. The one who believes in it will not be disturbed."

—Isaiah 28:16 (NASB)

The rain came down, the streams rose, and the winds blew and beat against that house; yet it did not fall, because it had its foundation on the rock.

—Matthew 7:25 (NIV)

lift

The work assignment seemed overwhelming. Why did I agree to do it? I complained to the Lord: "I don't have the right skill set. I don't have enough time. Help!" My mind raced from one worst-case scenario to another.

Unable to concentrate, I took a walk around a nearby lake. I paused to absorb the beauty of the water, the swans, the surrounding mountains. The Holy Spirit whispered to me, "Lift up your eyes. The Maker of these mountains will enable you to complete this task." Calmness washed over me, through me. As I continued my walk, a plan for tackling the task unfolded. "Thank You, Lord."

Lift. When tasks seem unmanageable, lift them to the Lord. When anxiety threatens your trust, lift it to the Prince of Peace. Every day, as often as necessary, lift.

—Denise Loock

Gracious God, I lift my concerns to You today. Amen.

Words to Pray On

I lift up my eyes to you, to you who sit enthroned in heaven.

—Psalm 123:1 (NIV)

I lift up my eyes to the mountains—where does my help come from? My help comes from the LORD, the Maker of heaven and earth. He will not let your foot slip—he who watches over you will not slumber; indeed, he who watches over Israel will neither slumber nor sleep.

—Psalm 121:1–4 (NIV)

Hear my cry for mercy as I call to you for help, as I lift up my hands toward your Most Holy Place.

—Psalm 28:2 (NIV)

not

I was scared and shaken after three trips to the hospital ER with severe chest pains. I was not afraid of death. As a believer in Christ Jesus, I knew heaven was my destination if I died. But I was scared for my children and frightened by the unknown, undiagnosed heart problem.

I asked my pastor if I could be anointed with oil and have the elders pray over me. Before the anointing, I read Psalm 16:8–9 (see opposite page), and an amazing peace filled me. I marked the date in the margin of my Bible, wrote the passage on index cards, and gave them to others who would pray with me. I was determined that I would *not* be shaken. I would *not* gaze at my circumstance; rather, I would fix my eyes on Jesus. I would put my hope and trust in God.

—Manette Kay

Father, the Holy Spirit is in me and Jesus sits at Your right hand. Therefore, I will not be shaken—my faith will remain strong. My heart is glad, and I will count my blessings. Amen.

Words to Pray On

I always let the Lord guide me. Because he is at my right hand, I will not be shaken. Therefore my heart is glad and my whole being rejoices; my body also rests securely.

—Psalm 16:8–9 (CSB)

When I am afraid, I will trust in you. In God, whose word I praise, in God I trust; I will not be afraid. What can mere mortals do to me?

—Psalm 56:3–4 (CSB)

The poor and the needy seek water, but there is none; their tongues are parched with thirst. I will answer them. I am the Lord, the God of Israel. I will not abandon them.

—Isaiah 41:17 (CSB)

confidence

When presented with uncertainties and impossibilities, my personality is to charge ahead, intent on figuring it out. My motto: Do enough of the right things, and it'll all work out. But whose confidence am I resting in? Who am I counting on? I would find far more peace if I turned first to the One who can make those impossibilities possible and the uncertainties certain—if I draw on His strength before my own strength fails.

No, I can't handle the crosses I'm asked to bear—loss, an uncertain future, caregiving—they're too heavy. But the Lord promises to help carry those crosses when I trust in Him. That's the key: trust!

Where I put my confidence makes all the difference in handling the hardest things in life. I fail when I trust in myself, but placing my confidence in Christ, trusting Him with my burdens, gives me the strength to finish my race well.

—Julie Sunne

Lord, help me trust You to help me carry my cross, placing my confidence in You, so I can finish my race well. Amen.

Words to Pray On

Do not be afraid of sudden terror or of the ruin of the wicked, when it comes, for the LORD will be your confidence and will keep your foot from being caught.
—Proverbs 3:25–26 (ESV)

Such is the confidence that we have through Christ toward God. Not that we are sufficient in ourselves to claim anything as coming from us, but our sufficiency is from God, who has made us sufficient to be ministers of a new covenant, not of the letter but of the Spirit.
—2 Corinthians 3:4–6 (ESV)

Is not your fear of God your confidence, and the integrity of your ways your hope?
—Job 4:6 (ESV)

eyes

My grown son called the other night, complaining of an irritation in his left eye. *It's no big deal. You'll get over it,* I thought dismissively. But aloud I suggested all the usual remedies: eye drops, flushing with water, a few hours' rest.

A couple of weeks later, he reported that the problem had not gone away. He'd visited an eye doctor, who diagnosed an ingrown eyelash but was unable to treat it. After 3 weeks trying to work with a patch covering his streaming, inflamed eye, he saw an oculo-plastic surgeon, who remedied the situation.

How easy it was for me to brush off his condition as insignificant, with my limited understanding and even more limited compassion. Though I can see well enough physically, the eyes of my heart often need healing from quick and insensitive judgments.

—Leslie McLeod

Jesus, my beloved Physician, I am grateful for Your kindness and power to heal not only physical blindness, but also my blindness to others' perspectives and needs. Help me to see those around me with eyes like Yours.

Words to Pray On

Why do you look at the speck of sawdust in your brother's eye and pay no attention to the plank in your own eye? How can you say to your brother, "Let me take the speck out of your eye," when all the time there is a plank in your own eye? You hypocrite, first take the plank out of your own eye, and then you will see clearly to remove the speck from your brother's eye.

—Matthew 7:3–5 (NIV)

Do you still not see or understand? Are your hearts hardened? Do you have eyes but fail to see, and ears but fail to hear?

—Mark 8:17–18 (NIV)

Once more Jesus put his hands on the man's eyes. Then his eyes were opened, his sight was restored, and he saw everything clearly.

—Mark 8:25 (NIV)

cacti

When we first moved to New Mexico, I noticed some weeds in our backyard. I proceeded to try to dig up these wild, prickly desert succulents and made a discovery. They are tenacious! Every wild desert plant that I've tried to remove has deep roots, which are needed to access and store water. And most have thorns or spikes to keep the predators away that would like to steal their water.

I have a lot of respect now for these desert plants and their survival skills. I want to imitate those deep roots in my relationship with God so that I can access His "living water." By nurturing that relationship, I know I will bolster my defenses and keep away our society's many predators—I hope without being prickly. I'm willing to share that water.

—Nancy Schrock

Lord, help me to have strength like the desert cacti and become a tenacious storer and provider of Your life-giving water.

Words to Pray On

When a Samaritan woman came to draw water, Jesus said to her, "Will you give me a drink?" (His disciples had gone into the town to buy food.)

The Samaritan woman said to him, "You are a Jew and I am a Samaritan woman. How can you ask me for a drink?" (For Jews do not associate with Samaritans.)

Jesus answered her, "If you knew the gift of God and who it is that asks you for a drink, you would have asked him and he would have given you living water."

"Sir," the woman said, "you have nothing to draw with and the well is deep. Where can you get this living water?..."

Jesus answered, "Everyone who drinks this water will be thirsty again, but whoever drinks the water I give them will never thirst. Indeed, the water I give them will become in them a spring of water welling up to eternal life."

—John 4:7–14 (NIV)

unshakable

I had moved to Southern California only a month ago, and already the ground was shaking beneath me. An early morning earthquake tossed me from my bed and out of a deep sleep, and I ran out into the court-yard of the small apartment building. Waves leaped out of the swimming pool as frightened neighbors scurried from their units, disheveled and blurry-eyed.

The window frame buckled, and a stream of ants, once content underground, marched up the wall like soldiers escaping their collapsed bunker. Everything around me was moving as I tried to keep steady—everything but the heavy iron chandelier that hung in the complex entryway. Though it swung in lazy circles, it remained intact and untouched. It seemed that all the things rooted on earth were being shaken, but not the light above.

How similar we are when life unexpectedly rattles us. May we always remember that our strength lies in our unshakable God.

—Kimberly Shumate

Father, thank You for providing me with an unmovable Rock on which to stand. Amen.

Words to Pray On

Heaven and earth will pass away, but my words will never pass away.

—Matthew 24:35 (NIV)

"Has not my hand made all these things, and so they came into being?" declares the Lord. "These are the ones I look on with favor: those who are humble and contrite in spirit, and who tremble at my word."

—Isaiah 66:2 (NIV)

My flesh and my heart may fail, but God is the strength of my heart and my portion forever.

—Psalm 73:26 (NIV)

teach

My writing mentor taught me that both writing and life itself are a dance, which is a little intimidating for someone like me who can't dance to save my life. I often feel like I'm forever taking one step forward and three steps back, tripping over my own feet and trying hard to not look like I'm still in middle school.

With writing, it's more like ten words written and twenty deleted. It's an awkward dance to put words to paper and craft them into a beautiful picture. Thankfully, I have a Teacher who knows every step, even my missteps, and He choreographs the most beautiful dance. I just have to follow His lead and allow Him to take my hand and show me the rhythm of His grace—the beauty of a life lived dancing with Him.

—Amy Wallace

Lord, teach me Your ways and help me learn the unforced rhythms of Your grace. Amen.

Words to Pray On

Walk with me and work with me—watch how I do it. Learn the unforced rhythms of grace. I won't lay anything heavy or ill-fitting on you. Keep company with me and you'll learn to live freely and lightly.

—Matthew 11:29–30 (MSG)

Moses said to the LORD, "Pardon your servant, Lord. I have never been eloquent, neither in the past nor since you have spoken to your servant. I am slow of speech and tongue."

The LORD said to him, "Who gave human beings their mouths? Who makes them deaf or mute? Who gives them sight or makes them blind? Is it not I, the LORD? Now go; I will help you speak and will teach you what to say."

—Exodus 4:10–12 (NIV)

reassurance

I zipped my windbreaker against the Alaskan chill and struggled to find my footing on rocks and sand. The conditions seemed fitting. This was supposed to be a vacation, but a broken relationship weighed heavily on my mind.

I hung my head, which forced my gaze downward to the smooth, Pacific Ocean rocks. I picked one up. It felt good in my hands.

"What happened to make this rock so smooth?" I asked myself and maybe God. I wondered how much pressure from wind and water had worn it down.

Then I spotted a heart-shaped rock! I sensed God reassuring me that my heart felt good in His hands too.

That heart rock now holds a place of honor on my dresser. It's a tangible reassurance from a hard walk on a rocky beach. And it reminds me that even in difficult circumstances, my heart can still beat for Him.

—Laurie Davies

Lord, when our eyes are downcast and our footing is unsteady, thank You for caring deeply about our hearts. Amen.

Words to Pray On

I will give you a new heart and put a new spirit in you;
I will remove from you your heart of stone and give
you a heart of flesh.

—Ezekiel 36:26 (NIV)

Create in me a pure heart, O God, and renew a
steadfast spirit within me. Do not cast me from your
presence or take your Holy Spirit from me. Restore
to me the joy of your salvation and grant me a willing
spirit, to sustain me.

—Psalm 51:10–12 (NIV)

Though you have made me see troubles, many and
bitter, you will restore my life again; from the depths
of the earth you will again bring me up. You will
increase my honor and comfort me once more.

—Psalm 71:20–21 (NIV)

fight

Ever feel like your cause was ignored? Your voice silenced? Your situation hopeless? Or have you perhaps faced a daunting enemy? Scripture tells us that the Israelites felt terrified as they fled from their captivity in Egypt. In their minds, they were facing a sure death from their pursuers. Moses told them to stand firm, be still, and prepare to see the deliverance that God would bring. In their wildest dreams, they could not have imagined what was about to take place.

In our world of position and prestige, we might feel like the Israelites—overpowered and without hope. Facing our enemies can be terrifying. However, the Bible reminds us that we have an all-powerful Savior who fights on our behalf, not only in the earthly realm that we can see with our eyes, but also against the spiritual forces of evil in the unseen heavenly realm. We need only to be still.

—Mindy Baker

Lord, thank You for rising up to fight for me. Quiet my heart and my mind in Your presence.

Words to Pray On

Moses answered the people, "Do not be afraid. Stand firm and you will see the deliverance the Lᴏʀᴅ will bring you today. The Egyptians you see today you will never see again. The Lᴏʀᴅ will fight for you, you need only to be still."

—Exodus 14:13–14 (NIV)

The Lᴏʀᴅ has driven out before you great and powerful nations; to this day no one has been able to withstand you. One of you routs a thousand, because the Lᴏʀᴅ your God fights for you, just as he promised.

—Joshua 23:9–10 (NIV)

For though we live in the world, we do not wage war as the world does. The weapons we fight with are not the weapons of the world.

—2 Corinthians 10:3–4 (NIV)

Nothing is so strong as gentleness, nothing so gentle as real strength.
—Saint Francis de Sales

carrier

Today, I took my "puppy," Choco, to the vet for his 1-year checkup, and I'm remembering the trip a year ago when I flew to another state to get him. At first he wasn't sure about me—until I gave him treats, and then we were buddies.

On the plane, he protested being in the carrier, and at 13 pounds, he was a bit cramped. He barked and howled like he was being tortured. The stewardess wouldn't let me take him out, so his howling continued—while I apologized to the woman whose seat he was under.

I think about all the times I was in a difficult situation and wanted out. Now, whenever I feel that way, I tell myself that God is carrying me to a new place, even if I don't know where or why. And like my puppy, who is now 74 pounds, I know I'll end up somewhere much better.

—Nancy Schrock

Lord, I know You will carry me through the turbulence and give me the strength for whatever tough situations I find myself in.

Words to Pray On

We can be so sure that every detail in our lives of love for God is worked into something good.
—Romans 8:28 (MSG)

Those who sow with tears will reap with songs of joy. Those who go out weeping, carrying seed to sow, will return with songs of joy, carrying sheaves with them.
—Psalm 126:5–6 (NIV)

Even to your old age and gray hairs I am he, I am he who will sustain you. I am he who made you and I will carry you; I will sustain you and I will rescue you.
—Isaiah 46:4 (NIV)

But you will cross the Jordan and settle in the land the LORD your God is giving you as an inheritance, and he will give you rest from all your enemies around you so that you will live in safety.
—Deuteronomy 12:10 (NIV)

face

Late one night, I turned over in bed and saw a light shine under the bedroom door. It disappeared and then shone again, as if a flashlight were sweeping back and forth. Terrified, I whispered, "Someone's in the house!" Before my husband could stir, I leaped from bed and crouched at the door. Our three-month-old baby lay asleep across the hall, and my mama-bear instincts launched into high gear.

The culprit turned out to be a faulty light bulb in the living room. We thought we'd turned the lamp completely off, but the bulb filament continued to flicker. I breathed a sigh of relief that my fears were groundless.

It wasn't wrong to be afraid, but looking back I realized that God had helped me act despite those fears. Some things I have no control over, but with a mighty God at my side, I can face situations that frighten me and overcome them.

—Tracy Crump

Lord, walk beside me and help me face down my fears, knowing I can trust You.

Words to Pray On

Whenever I am afraid, I will trust in You. In God (I will praise His word), in God I have put my trust; I will not fear. What can flesh do to me?

—Psalm 56:3–4 (NKJV)

For God has not given us a spirit of fear, but of power and of love and of a sound mind.

—2 Timothy 1:7 (NKJV)

And David said to his son Solomon, "Be strong and of good courage, and do it; do not fear nor be dismayed, for the LORD God—my God—will be with you. He will not leave you nor forsake you, until you have finished all the work for the service of the house of the LORD."

—1 Chronicles 28:20 (NKJV)

crumbs

I once had a teacher who early in life became an orphan. He was raised by his grandmother and great-aunt during World War II. In his country, there was much danger but little food, and even a slice of bread was a luxury. At the end of each meal, his grandmother raked clean the oilcloth covering the kitchen table, collecting any crumbs, each a life-saving ingredient of another meal.

I was born into abundance. Entire meals, left almost untouched, were chucked into the trash. I grew up believing the plenty of 3 meals a day was my due. I could not imagine stooping for a crumb.

Today I ask myself—though I have no answer—could I shed my pride and beg a saving crumb from the table of the Lord, as the Greek woman did for her demon-ridden daughter in Mark 7?

—Lou Anthony

Dear Jesus, make me as bold and as humble as the Greek woman begging for crumbs for the daughter she loves. Teach me her bold belief, her courage when I pray. Amen.

Words to Pray On

As soon as she heard about him, a woman whose little daughter was possessed by an impure spirit came and fell at his feet. The woman was a Greek, born in Syrian Phoenicia. She begged Jesus to drive the demon out of her daughter. "First let the children eat all they want," he told her, "for it is not right to take the children's bread and toss it to the dogs." "Lord," she replied, "even the dogs under the table eat the children's crumbs." Then he told her, "For such a reply, you may go. The demon has left your daughter." She went home and found her child lying on the bed, and the demon gone.

—Mark 7:25–30 (NIV)

sufficient

Being a leader in the church means I need to make God look good. Right? No fear. Check. Never doubt or worry over things outside of my control. Check. Always in control of my reactions and emotions. Check. Because I'm a follower of Christ, I often believe I need to meet everyone's expectations of being a put-together Christian. At the root of this dilemma is pride.

Pride says I should be able to implement the perfect strategy to build a team of knowledgeable volunteers and staff. Pride says I shouldn't allow the people I lead to see me struggle openly after a scuffle in the car with my husband on the way to church. The truth is, God's power is sufficient.

When I feel weak, may it remind me He is sufficient. When pride tricks me into believing I should be doing better than I am, may I remember He is sufficient. His grace is enough. We don't make God look bad because we are weak and in desperate need—we illuminate that He is sufficient.

—Ashley Moore

Lord, thank You that when I am weak, others see Your strength. Thank You that You are sufficient. Amen.

Words to Pray On

But he said to me, "My grace is sufficient for you, for my power is made perfect in weakness." Therefore I will boast all the more gladly about my weaknesses, so that Christ's power may rest on me. That is why, for Christ's sake, I delight in weaknesses, in insults, in hardships, in persecutions, in difficulties. For when I am weak, then I am strong.

—2 Corinthians 12:9–10 (NIV)

You are the most excellent of men and your lips have been anointed with grace, since God has blessed you forever.

—Psalm 45:2 (NIV)

Finally, be strong in the Lord and in his mighty power.

—Ephesians 6:10 (NIV)

up

We recently moved from a hundred-year-old house in the city to 4 wide-open acres in the country. In the city, the night sky was blurred by a plethora of lights scattered throughout the downtown. In the country, however, the chalkboard sky acts as a backdrop for the stars to shine their best and brightest.

Sometimes circumstances can blur the reality of God's presence. Worries, fears, and the "what if" questions creep up and hold our peace of mind hostage. But when we choose to step away and look up instead of around, our spiritual eyes come into focus. We're able to see God's goodness, constant care, and power more clearly.

A heavenwardly shift in perspective can become the backdrop for God's peace to shine brightly in our hearts as well as our darkened world.

—Cathy Baker

Lord, help me to shine like the stars for Your glory today. Amen.

Words to Pray On

Look up into the heavens. Who created all the stars?
He brings them out like an army, one after another,
calling each by its name. Because of his great power
and incomparable strength, not a single one is missing.
—Isaiah 40:26 (NLT)

Be gracious to me, O Lord, for to you do I cry all the
day. Gladden the soul of your servant, for to you, O
Lord, do I lift up my soul. For you, O Lord, are good
and forgiving, abounding in steadfast love to all who
call upon you.
—Psalm 86:3–5 (ESV)

resurrection

It was one of those days. I had a head cold that sapped all my energy and patience. Unfortunately, mothers of young children can't take sick days. We just have to push through.

One of my kids did something wrong, and I completely overreacted. As I screamed and yelled, a heavy feeling settled over our kitchen. Then my little daughter came over, hugged my leg, and simply said, "I love you, Mommy." Immediately, everything was OK.

Yes, those arms wrapped around my leg were my daughter's, but they were Jesus's too. He works through everyone and everything, and He sees each one of us, just like He saw the widow in Luke 7 (see the scripture on the facing page). Out of compassion for her, He resurrected her son. Out of compassion for me, He worked through my daughter and resurrected me, giving me the patience and energy I needed to get through the remainder of the day.

—Claire McGarry

Lord, remind me that You always stand at the ready to resurrect me with Your compassion. Amen.

Words to Pray On

As he approached the town gate, a dead person was being carried out—the only son of his mother, and she was a widow. And a large crowd from the town was with her. When the Lord saw her, his heart went out to her, and he said, "Don't cry." Then he went up and touched the bier they were carrying him on, and the bearers stood still. He said, "Young man, I say to you, get up!" The dead man sat up and began to talk, and Jesus gave him back to his mother.

—Luke 7:12–15 (NIV)

Praise be to the God and Father of our Lord Jesus Christ! In his great mercy he has given us new birth into a living hope through the resurrection of Jesus Christ from the dead.

—1 Peter 1:3 (NIV)

quilt

Some years ago, my mother gifted me with a hand-made quilt made entirely of random scraps of cloth. The random pieces were arranged and sewn together into a stunning log cabin design.

Just as the quilt is a beautiful whole constructed of different individual parts, so are we and our particular gifts. Our uniqueness is a reminder that God crafted a world of people with varying gifts, each contributing to the pattern of a whole, each created to reflect Him and His glory to a fraying world with threadbare hope.

We each have a place and purpose in this world as we use our gifts and talents not just for their own sake or only for ourselves, but as part of a larger, magnificent whole. All the while, God is stitching together a beautiful tapestry, placing each piece, each life, perfectly in the pattern He is designing.

—Prasanta Verma

Dear Lord, thank You for the unique gifts You have given to each person. Please help me to wisely use the gifts You have given me. Amen.

Words to Pray On

For we are God's handiwork, created in Christ Jesus to do good works, which God prepared in advance for us to do.

—Ephesians 2:10 (NIV)

There are different kinds of gifts, but the same Spirit distributes them. There are different kinds of service, but the same Lord. There are different kinds of working, but in all of them and in everyone it is the same God at work. Now to each one the manifestation of the Spirit is given for the common good.

—1 Corinthians 12:4–7 (NIV)

contentment

One great line in a Bob Dylan song says, "She's an artist / she don't look back."* In college, I took a painting class where the instructor referenced these lyrics as a truism. The instructor said that a good painter, one who wants to advance in creativity, will never surround himself with his own paintings. That would mean he was looking backward, stuck in a certain style, stifling his creativity.

I'm reminded of Dylan's words and the wisdom of my art instructor when I'm around someone who lives in the past, always recalling the glory days of their youth. That's a dangerous trap to fall into, because we become stuck focusing backward on the past instead of enjoying the present moment, contented and thankful for what God has provided. I don't want to miss out on the blessings and tender mercies of today by longing for the past.

—Dale R. Yancy

Dear Lord, let my contentment be in You. I want to enjoy Your presence and experience the blessings You have for me this day. Amen.

---

*"She Belongs to Me," lyrics by Bob Dylan, © Universal Music Publishing Group.

Words to Pray On

But godliness with contentment is great gain, for we brought nothing into the world, and we cannot take anything out of the world.

—1 Timothy 6:6–7 (ESV)

Not that I am speaking of being in need, for I have learned in whatever situation I am to be content. I know how to be brought low, and I know how to abound. In any and every circumstance, I have learned the secret of facing plenty and hunger, abundance and need.

—Philippians 4:11–12 (ESV)

overcome

During the midst of seminary study came the words that no one wants to hear: "It's cancer." I knew this meant taking at least one semester off, which was not what I wanted at all!

I wasn't angry at God. I just didn't want to talk to Him. A friend suggested that, instead of forcing my usual prayer routine, I take my morning cup of coffee and sit with God where I normally would pray. It felt uncomfortable, but I tried anyway.

Within a few weeks, I was on my knees, praying for God's strength to enter my heart and overcome whatever needed to be overcome in me—physically, emotionally, and spiritually—so that I could walk through this difficulty with a dignity that would lead others to Him.

All I had to do was take the action to show up, and God did the rest, supporting me through treatment and into my eventual remission. He always overcomes!

—Jessica L. Morris

God, I pray that You will help me focus on Your strength in me to overcome all the things of this world that bring me trouble throughout this day.

Words to Pray On

I have told you these things, so that in me you may have peace. In this world you will have trouble. But take heart! I have overcome the world.

—John 16:33 (NIV)

Then the man said, "Your name will no longer be Jacob, but Israel, because you have struggled with God and with humans and have overcome."

—Genesis 32:28 (NIV)

In him was life, and that life was the light of all mankind. The light shines in the darkness, and the darkness has not overcome it.

—John 1:4–5 (NIV)

sacred

After rushing through my morning prayer and dressing quickly, I bolted to my car. I made it with barely enough time to board the train heading downtown. I felt strings of guilt tugging at my heart. My new job was an unexpected blessing, but now I felt rushed in the mornings because of my longer commute, and yearned for more sacred time with God. Sitting on that train, I quieted my thoughts and began meditating on the word *sacred*.

Time and space spent with God is sacred, whether it happens in the quiet of our home, at church, or sitting on a train roaring to its next stop. Reframing my perspective of mornings on the train shifted the direction of the day. It changed from being an obstacle to my fellowship with God to becoming an opportunity dedicated to expanding my time with Him. The guilty feelings departed as peace settled on the altar of my heart, filling me with the assurance received from being in His sacred presence.

—Gwendolyn Burton

Father, help me to observe any time and space I spend in Your presence as sacred. Amen.

Words to Pray On

Now my eyes will be open and my ears attentive to
the prayer offered in this place.

—2 Chronicles 7:15 (NIV)

Don't you know that you yourselves are God's temple
and that God's Spirit dwells in your midst?

—1 Corinthians 3:16 (NIV)

Now devote your heart and soul to seeking the Lord
your God. Begin to build the sanctuary of the Lord God.

—1 Chronicles 22:19 (NIV)

And God said, "Let there be lights in the vault of the
sky to separate the day from the night, and let them
serve as signs to mark sacred times, and days and
years, and let them be lights in the vault of the sky to
give light on the earth." And it was so.

—Genesis 1:14–15 (NIV)

art

I filled with dread any time my two daughters came home with school art assignments. I can barely draw a stick figure. Our neighbor Ilene, an artist and potter, was always eager to help out, but I never wanted to attempt any art on my own because it felt so intimidating.

On a recent trip to New Mexico, however, I toured the home of renowned artist Georgia O'Keeffe. The guide told us her philosophy about art: simply filling a page or a space in a beautiful way. Suddenly, art seemed more approachable. And what if I extended that idea to everyday life and asked myself, *What can I do today to make life more beautiful for those around me*? A kind word to a harried stranger or walking the dog for the tired new parents next door might color the world in a lovely shade.

—Mary Hix

Holy Artist, show me ways to make my life a work of art that pleases You and colors the world in a beautiful way. Amen.

Words to Pray On

Your beauty should not come from outward adornment, such as elaborate hairstyles and the wearing of gold jewelry or fine clothes. Rather, it should be that of your inner self, the unfading beauty of a gentle and quiet spirit, which is of great worth in God's sight.

—1 Peter 3:3–4 (NIV)

By wisdom a house is built, and through understanding it is established; through knowledge its rooms are filled with rare and beautiful treasures.

—Proverbs 24:3–4 (NIV)

How beautiful on the mountains are the feet of those who bring good news, who proclaim peace, who bring good tidings, who proclaim salvation, who say to Zion, "Your God reigns!"

—Isaiah 52:7 (NIV)

pleasing

I try to keep everyone happy. Every day I juggle a million things to make sure that everyone around me is OK, and some days it seems like I pick up a thousand more. While some of that is good, some is not what God calls me to.

When the children's church director asked me to teach on Sundays, I said yes. I knew God was calling me to a season of rest, but I didn't want to let the director down. I spent the next season running ragged and weary, wondering why I couldn't get a handle on things.

We are called, as Colossians 1:10 tells us, to "walk worthy of the Lord, fully pleasing Him" (NKJV). When we are hyper-focused on pleasing those around us, like I was when I said yes to helping in children's church, we can miss what God is calling us to do. Instead, we can choose to live lives that allow us to be fruitful and grow, and give ourselves the space to be open to God's nudges.

—Rebecca Hastings

Lord, help me live a life that is pleasing to You and Your ways before all else. Amen.

Words to Pray On

We are asking that you may be filled with the knowledge of his will in all wisdom and spiritual understanding, so that you may walk worthy of the Lord, fully pleasing to him: bearing fruit in every good work and growing in the knowledge of God.

—Colossians 1:9–10 (CSB)

Therefore, brothers and sisters, in view of the mercies of God, I urge you to present your bodies as a living sacrifice, holy and pleasing to God; this is your true worship. Do not be conformed to this age, but be transformed by the renewing of your mind, so that you may discern what is the good, pleasing, and perfect will of God.

—Romans 12:1–2 (CSB)

breath

When I take a moment to pause and notice my breath, it always reminds me of God. There is something about a breath that is so cleansing and calming, creating a nearly tangible peace. And there are so many times we take the gift of breath for granted—inhaling and exhaling without thought of the miracle we're participating in.

When I'm in the midst of a busy day of teaching and it seems like every student is calling my name, I don't have a chance to remember how the Almighty chooses to sustain me moment by moment. But when I pause—when I take a few moments to rest, breathing deep—I can feel the Lord wipe away the cares of the day. He soothes my mind with the healing balm of peace. What wonders He can work when we separate ourselves from the busyness of life…and just breathe.

—Haley V. Craft

Father, help me be intentional in finding times to pause and breathe, resting in You and giving thanks for the miracle of life. Amen.

Words to Pray On

Then the LORD God formed a man from the dust of the ground and breathed into his nostrils the breath of life, and the man became a living being.
—Genesis 2:7 (NIV)

The Spirit of God has made me; the breath of the Almighty gives me life.
—Job 33:4 (NIV)

Again Jesus said, "Peace be with you! As the Father has sent me, I am sending you." And with that he breathed on them and said, "Receive the Holy Spirit."
—John 20:21–22 (NIV)

lavish

I come from a long line of flower-lovers. From a young age, I was taught how to watch for crocus shoots in early spring, to coax nectar from honeysuckle blossoms, and to gently peek beneath the leaves of may-apple plants to look for blossoms. I learned many of their names—snapdragon, butter-and-eggs, forget-me-nots. But not even my mother and grandmother knew them all.

Do you know how many species of flowers there are? Over 300,000! God could have made just one or two kinds. Even ten would have been generous. But 300,000? That's lavish. He is a lavish, over-the-top, more-than-we-could-ever-imagine God. And His lavishness reaches beyond flowers. He is lavish in His love. Lavish in His grace. Lavish in His provision. Don't be afraid to ask for more from God—His generosity is lavish, too.

—Kate Rietema

Lord, thank You for being lavish. Amen.

Words to Pray On

Now to him who is able to do immeasurably more than all we ask or imagine, according to his power that is at work within us, to him be glory in the church and in Christ Jesus throughout all generations, forever and ever!

—Ephesians 3:20–21 (NIV)

See what great love the Father has lavished on us, that we should be called children of God! And that is what we are! The reason the world does not know us is that it did not know him. Dear friends, now we are children of God, and what we will be has not yet been made known. But we know that when Christ appears, we shall be like him, for we shall see him as he is.

—1 John 3:1–2 (NIV)

Some of us think holding
on makes us strong;
but sometimes it is letting go.
—Hermann Hesse

pursue

We could not give up. God had called us to adopt three children from Haiti and we'd been in the process for years. We knew them by name. We'd held them in our arms. They were ours. In a horrific turn of events, a corrupt agent stole our files. We moved heaven and earth and at times risked life and limb to get our files returned. This suburban housewife became detective, bold advocate, passionate pursuer. We retrieved our files and completed the adoption.

How much more does our God come for us! God pursues us with divine precision and unrelenting focus. He pursues our hearts. He never gives up. He moves heaven and earth, uses all of creation, woos us with His care, and fights off anyone else who would try to kidnap our hearts. He will never give up. We are His. He loves us and will abandon all else to capture our love.

—Elsa Kok Colopy

Lord, help me to see how You pursue me. You love me so well. Don't let me miss it. Thank You for coming for me!

Words to Pray On

Or suppose a woman has ten silver coins and loses one. Doesn't she light a lamp, sweep the house and search carefully until she finds it?

—Luke 15:8 (NIV)

Whoever of you loves life and desires to see many good days, keep your tongue from evil and your lips from telling lies. Turn from evil and do good; seek peace and pursue it.

—Psalm 34:12–14 (NIV)

Whoever pursues righteousness and love finds life, prosperity, and honor.

—Proverbs 21:21 (NIV)

hands

The scars on my mother-in-law's hands testified to her labor. Carolyn raised five sons and ran a farm alone after the death of her 40-year-old husband. She worked from dawn until midnight to mend barbed wire fences and complete other manual-labor chores.

Six days a week, she herded cows, ironed shirts, and patted out biscuits without complaint. On Sundays, Bible in hand, she ushered her boys into a pew at their tiny country church. Whether she baled hay, bandaged knees, or worshipped her Lord, Carolyn's hands accomplished the work God assigned to her.

What will God call you to do today? Hold the hand of a grieving widow? Write an encouraging note? Or pick up a hammer to mend a fence? Each day, let's seek God's will in prayer and ask Him to bless the work of our hands.

—Jeannie Waters

Heavenly Father, lead me to use my hands to honor You and meet the needs of those You place on my path. Amen.

Words to Pray On

And let the beauty of the Lᴏʀᴅ our God be upon us, and establish the work of our hands for us; yes, establish the work of our hands.

—Psalm 90:17 (NKJV)

But you, be strong and do not let your hands be weak, for your work shall be rewarded!

—2 Chronicles 15:7 (NKJV)

But we urge you, brethren, that you increase more and more; that you also aspire to lead a quiet life, to mind your own business, and to work with your own hands, as we commanded you, that you may walk properly toward those who are outside, and that you may lack nothing.

—1 Thessalonians 4:10–12 (NKJV)

see

I was just one step away from being legally blind. The lenses in my glasses were a half-inch thick. After much searching, I found an eye doctor willing to do vision correction surgery for me. To my disappointment, the procedure didn't give me 20/20 vision. I still needed glasses. "Give thanks in all circumstances," says our Lord. "How do I do that?" I wondered out loud. Often.

But I could now have much thinner lenses. That meant I could pick pretty frames instead of settling for whatever frame could hold the thick lenses. To remember to be thankful for that, I popped the old half-inch lenses out of their frame, drilled a small hole in each one, and tied them together with a ribbon that I hung on my desk.

Now, unfortunately, an unrelated issue is causing me to go blind. I see my old lenses, and I will still be thankful.

—Pamela Haskin

O Lord, even when circumstances are hard for me, please help me see a way to be thankful.

Words to Pray On

Rejoice always, pray continually, give thanks in all circumstances; for this is God's will for you in Christ Jesus.

—1 Thessalonians 5:16–18 (NIV)

Give thanks to the LORD, for he is good; his love endures forever. Cry out, "Save us, God our Savior; gather us and deliver us from the nations, that we may give thanks to your holy name, and glory in your praise."

—1 Chronicles 16:34–35 (NIV)

Enter his gates with thanksgiving and his courts with praise; give thanks to him and praise his name. For the LORD is good and his love endures forever; his faithfulness continues through all generations.

—Psalm 100:4–5 (NIV)

worth

When I was 14, my mother passed away and my ambitious aunt and underachieving uncle took me in. My uncle's drunken stupors triggered a barrage of negative words directed at me, letting me know I'd never amount to anything. These negative words really hurt and impacted my self-confidence and sense of worth.

Since my youth, the healing journey I've been on has come to center around two personal truths. First, people who are in pain often hurt others as a form of coping. Understanding this has put a protective shield into my hands I call empathy.

Second, my worth is not measured today by the words of those who hurt but by the words of the Healer. God says I'm the beloved, fearfully and wonderfully made, a light to the world, and more than a conqueror. His scriptural messages to me are a transfusion of confidence that defines my worth. I speak them daily over my life.

—Kenneth Avon White

Father, help me never lose sight of the fact that Your words validate my worth and promising destiny.

Words to Pray On

But you are a chosen generation, a royal priesthood, a holy nation, His own special people, that you may proclaim the praises of Him who called you out of darkness into His marvelous light.

—1 Peter 2:9 (NKJV)

Your beauty should not come from outward adornment, such as elaborate hairstyles and the wearing of gold jewelry or fine clothes. Rather, it should be that of your inner self, the unfading beauty of a gentle and quiet spirit, which is of great worth in God's sight.

—1 Peter 3:3–4 (NIV)

Is it fitting to say to a king, "You are worthless," and to nobles, "You are wicked"? Yet He is not partial to princes, nor does He regard the rich more than the poor; for they are all the work of His hands.

—Job 34:18–19 (NKJV)

immediate

My son and I both suffer from the same ailment. The official medical term for it is "trying to figure out all of life's problems in the next 5 minutes syndrome."

One day my son woke up and was immediately preoccupied with all the worries facing him, present and future. I took a deep breath with him, rubbed his back, and said, "All I want you to focus on right now is getting out of bed."

Life can be so overwhelming that we miss simply being in the present. God's hope is for a *future* with Him, but He also walks with us *now*. The word *immediate* actually means "without medium or mediation," and it is because of Jesus's death and resurrection that we have this immediate access to our Heavenly Father. He may feel far away at times, but He is with you at this very moment, giving you peace and grace, and He will be with you every step of the way.

—Juliette Alvey

Lord, Your immediate, loving presence is with me at all times, especially when worries about the present and future threaten to overwhelm me. Thank You for never leaving my side. Amen.

Words to Pray On

Immediately he spoke to them and said, "Take courage! It is I. Don't be afraid."

—Mark 6:50 (NIV)

And I will ask the Father, and he will give you another advocate to help you and be with you forever—the Spirit of truth. The world cannot accept him, because it neither sees him nor knows him. But you know him, for he lives with you and will be in you.

—John 14:16–17 (NIV)

And surely I am with you always, to the very end of the age.

—Matthew 28:20 (NIV)

The LORD your God is with you, the Mighty Warrior who saves. He will take great delight in you; in his love he will no longer rebuke you, but will rejoice over you with singing.

—Zephaniah 3:17 (NIV)

cairn

A beautiful photo of eight colorful stones, stacked from largest to smallest, caught my attention and made me pause. *Unbelievable, I thought. How do these polished flat stones support each other?*

Cairn is a Scottish Gaelic word from the fifteenth century, but the practice of creating these distinctive stacks of stones goes back to prehistoric times. But cairns are far from mere piles of rock. There is something spiritual in their design. The large base provides strength to the rest of the structure, and each of the carefully placed smaller stones support one another. A visible balancing act that always reminds me of a life of faith, where God is our rock and strength.

We may feel like the tiny top stone at some points during our lives—precariously balanced and ready to topple at any moment—but with the support of faith, family, and friends, we will find strength during our "rocky" times.

Remember: A tiny stone blessed with God's grace gave David the strength to slay a giant.

—Mary Bredel Fike

Lord, we know there is strength in numbers. Bless us with the grace to be there for others.

Words to Pray On

So Jacob took a stone and set it up as a pillar. He said to his relatives, "Gather some stones." So they took stones and piled them in a heap, and they ate there by the heap. . . . Laban said, "This heap is a witness between you and me today."

—Genesis 31:45–46, 48 (NIV)

The LORD is my rock, my fortress and my deliverer; my God is my rock, in whom I take refuge, my shield and the horn of my salvation, my stronghold.

—Psalm 18:2 (NIV)

Joshua also set up another pile of twelve stones in the middle of the Jordan, at the place where the priests who carried the Ark of the Covenant were standing. And they are there to this day.

—Joshua 4:9 (NLT)

paralyzed

A skilled therapist once helped me realize I had become paralyzed when it came to making any kind of decisions. "It's not surprising, if you think about what you've been through!" she offered.

The previous 2 years had been a string of unexpected course corrections. I'd agonized over a perfect birth-plan, and nothing went right...in fact, it went very wrong. We'd made a hard decision about moving, going as far as packing and making renovations to the new place—until it fell through. A career change led to less stability rather than more.

So, to protect itself from more disappointment and stress, my brain just refused to move when asked to make even a simple decision. As I healed, I continued to find other atrophied areas in my heart. Unanswered prayer silencing my urge to pray, or a scornful word freezing my willingness to forgive. More things to lower through the roof—as the paralyzed man's friends did for him—and lay at Jesus's feet.

—Sarah Greek

Cast out all fear today and give me the strength to reach for Your hand, believing I will walk strong and whole. Amen.

Words to Pray On

Then—look! Some men came carrying a paralyzed man on a sleeping mat. They tried to push through the crowd to Jesus but couldn't reach him. So they went up on the room above him, took off some tiles, and lowered the sick man down into the crowd, still on his sleeping mat, right in front of Jesus.... Turning to the paralyzed man, he commanded, "Pick up your stretcher and go on home, for you are healed!"

—Luke 5:18–19, 24 (TLB)

The Lord says, "Don't be afraid! "Don't be paralyzed by this mighty army! For the battle is not yours, but God's!"

—2 Chronicles 20:15 (TLB)

encouragement

My friend Marisa is one of my favorite people. She has the gift of encouragement. She asks about non-superficial things in my life, and when I answer, she really listens to what I have to say. She doesn't try to minimize my challenges by saying something like, "All kids are difficult." But more than that, her words come home to roost in my heart because they're delivered with enthusiasm, with direct eye contact, and with a broad smile. As she speaks, she touches my shoulder to make sure I haven't missed her support and encouragement.

As I thought about Marisa, I wondered what I could do to convey that same sense of encouragement to my loved ones. From then on, I started to pay attention to my voice quality, body language, facial expressions, and gestures, looking for ways to build up the people around me.

—Becky Hofstad

Lord, I pray that You'd help me to lift up the people in my life with enthusiasm so that they feel encouraged.

Words to Pray On

In the past you have encouraged many people; you have strengthened those were weak. Your words have supported those who were falling; you encouraged those with shaky knees.

—Job 4:3–4 (NLT)

Then the one who looked like a man touched me again, and I felt my strength returning. "Don't be afraid," he said, "for you are very precious to God. Peace! Be encouraged! Be strong!" As he spoke these words to me, I suddenly felt stronger and said to him, "Please speak to me, my lord, for you have strengthened me."

—Daniel 10:18–19 (NLT)

view

From a commonsense perspective, our family's move to another state seemed foolish. Neither my husband nor I had a job in the new city. No family lived nearby. People asked us, "Why are you moving where you don't know anyone?"

We answered, "We're sure God wants us to do it." God had made our path clear. Our children had chosen to attend universities in that state, and He aligned circumstances to clear the way for us to go.

Whenever anxiety arose during the transition I prayed, "Give me Your view, Lord. Don't let me get caught up in what others see—or think they're seeing. I want to see what You see."

Although the first 2 years after our move were stressful, God has continually confirmed we made the right decision. My husband and I are using our God-given skills in multiple ways in our new church and community.

So much depends on our vantage point. When the view from earth challenges your faith, ask God to provide His view.

—Denise Loock

Lord, give me Your view on the situation that's causing me to question Your good plan for me. Amen.

Words to Pray On

A discerning person keeps wisdom in view, but a fool's eyes wander to the ends of the earth.

—Proverbs 17:24 (NIV)

Let God hurry; let him hasten his work so that we may see it. The plan of the Holy One of Israel—let it approach, let it come into view, so that we may know it.

—Isaiah 5:19 (NIV)

They are from the world and therefore speak from the viewpoint of the world, and the world listens to them. We are from God, and whoever knows God listens to us.

—1 John 4:5–6 (NIV)

crossing

There are seventeen water crossings on the trail we're hiking. Some are hardly a trickle, and my kids splash right through. But one river has a log bridge spanning its banks, suspended 5 feet above the cascading water. Our sons eagerly cross and run ahead on the opposite side. My husband holds our youngest's hand and helps her balance. I hesitate, alone now on my side of the river. The moving water plays tricks on my eyes. My knees, right along with my resolve, go weak. I place a foot on the log, only to fearfully pull it back. Finally, looking away from the water's movement and to the stationary opposite end of the log, I cross over.

I picture that log often when life's circumstances feel as fluid and dizzying as the river. Shifting focus from all the moving pieces of life and fixing my eyes on Jesus, who does not change, I'm able to cross over any obstacle.

— Eryn Lynum

Dear Lord, when life is dizzying, draw my attention to Your steadfast ways. Help me cross over obstacles and press forward in Your strength.

Words to Pray On

Then you will go on your way in safety, and your foot will not stumble.

—Proverbs 3:23 (NIV)

Therefore, since we are surrounded by such a great cloud of witnesses, let us throw off everything that hinders and the sin that so easily entangles. And let us run with perseverance the race marked out for us, fixing our eyes on Jesus, the pioneer and perfecter of faith. For the joy set before him he endured the cross, scorning its shame, and sat down at the right hand of the throne of God.

—Hebrews 12:1–2 (NIV)

incomparable

I pulled nervously on my swimsuit strap as I entered the pool area. I couldn't help but size up my competition at this Masters Swim Meet. I despaired as I saw many swimmers who were younger and fitter than I was. Comparing my out-of-shape body to theirs did nothing for my confidence.

But then I reminded myself of the progress I'd made in the 3 months since I had begun training. Sure, I wasn't in tip-top shape, but I was stronger. Other swimmers were supportive and encouraging. I reminded myself that God had made me just the way I am for a purpose. I didn't have to compare myself to anyone else.

Each of us has to do our best in whatever God has planned for us in life. "Incomparable" can be our prayer as we stop comparing ourselves to others and enjoy how God has made us.

—Robyn Mulder

Lord, help me be grateful for how You've made me. Remind me that I don't need to compare myself with anyone else. Amen.

Words to Pray On

Each one should test their own actions. Then they can take pride in themselves alone, without comparing themselves to someone else, for each one should carry their own load.

—Galatians 6:4–5 (NIV)

We do not dare to classify or compare ourselves with some who commend themselves. When they measure themselves by themselves and compare themselves with themselves, they are not wise.

—2 Corinthians 10:12 (NIV)

I praise you because I am fearfully and wonderfully made; your works are wonderful, I know that full well.

—Psalm 139:14 (NIV)

boldness

Paralyzed by the thought of what an acceptance letter might mean, I hesitated to send the query. What if the editor actually assigned me a story and I couldn't do it? I felt called to write and share messages of God's hope, but feelings of inadequacy and fear always stopped me from following through. *How can I effectively write for the Lord?* I wondered. *I agonize over every word. I think my writings never measure up to others'. I question whether I have anything to add to the conversation or time to follow through. I'll just end up letting them down when I fail to deliver.*

Then one morning I read 1Thessalonians 2:2 (see opposite page). The short phrase "boldness in our God" jumped out at me, and conviction gripped my heart. I was not doing this alone. If I relied on my own strength, I was doomed, but in Christ, I could do anything He called me to. It was past time to obey, trust, and surrender. With God leading the way, I could exchange fear for boldness and step forward in confidence, clicking Send as I go.

—Julie Sunne

Lord, embolden me in all You call me to do, reminding me I'm not alone and giving me the confidence to carry out Your plan. Amen.

Words to Pray On

But though we had already suffered and been shamefully treated at Philippi, as you know, we had boldness in our God to declare to you the gospel of God in the midst of much conflict.

—1 Thessalonians 2:2 (ESV)

"And now, Lord, look upon their threats and grant to your servants to continue to speak your word with all boldness, while you stretch out your hand to heal, and signs are wonders are performed through the name of your holy servant Jesus." And when they had prayed, the place in which they were gathered together was shaken, and they were all filled with the Holy Spirit and continued to speak the word of God with boldness.

—Acts 4:29–31 (ESV)

link

Five years ago, we heard that our son's 19-year-old girlfriend was pregnant. Through a process of prayer and counsel, we agreed to help with the baby's care so that they could keep him and raise him. We weren't sure exactly what we were getting into, but we knew that we had a strong faith community that would come alongside all of us in support.

From donations of baby furniture and accessories to a baby shower to monetary gifts to help this young couple, each of our friends was a vital link in the chain of God's love that binds us to His heart. Without the help of the body of Christ, we might never have gotten the joy of helping to raise our beautiful grandson. We are grateful for every link in that chain.

—Stephanie Reeves

Father God, You have made us for community. There is no greater picture of Your love for us than our love for others. Thank You for the links that connect us, for the ties that bind us, for the love that flows from Your heart to ours. In Jesus's name I pray. Amen.

Words to Pray On

Two are better than one, because they have a good reward for their toil. For if they fall, one will lift up his fellow. But woe to him who is alone when he falls and has not another to lift him up! Again, if two lie together, they keep warm, but how can one keep warm alone? And though a man might prevail against one who is alone, two will withstand him—a threefold cord is not quickly broken.

—Ecclesiastes 4:9–12 (ESV)

Bear one another's burdens, and so fulfill the law of Christ.

—Galatians 6:2 (ESV)

A new commandment I give to you, that you love one another: just as I have loved you, you also are to love one another. By this all people will know that you are my disciples, if you have love for one another.

—John 13:34–35 (ESV)

rock

My dad's name is Peter. My mom often jokes that Dad embodies all the character traits of the apostle for whom he is named—both the good traits *and the bad*. Like Peter the apostle, Dad is very passionate, but sometimes that passion can make him a bit of a hothead. Nevertheless, he's the rock of our family, the one on whom his wife and four girls can depend.

Jesus knew that Simon had a lot of maturing to do even when he surnamed him Peter, "the rock." And yet He gave him the name anyway, because He already believed in the strong, rocklike leader he'd later become.

Whenever you doubt who you are or what you're meant to be, know that God—the King of heaven and earth—believes in you. Even when you can't see the great person you will become, God does—and He will see you right to the end.

—Roma Maitlall

Lord, thank You for seeing the potential in me and forming me into the strong, tough-as-a-rock person You meant me to be.

Words to Pray On

"But what about you?" he asked. "Who do you say I am?" Simon Peter answered, "You are the Messiah, the Son of the living God." Jesus replied, "Blessed are you, Simon son of Jonah, for this was not revealed to you by flesh and blood, but by my Father in heaven. And I tell you that you are Peter, and on this rock I will build my church, and the gates of Hades will not overcome it."

—Matthew 16:15–18 (NIV)

Therefore everyone who hears these words of mine and puts them into practice is like a wise man who built his house on the rock. The rain came down, the streams rose, and the winds blew and beat against that house; yet it did not fall, because it had its foundation on the rock.

—Matthew 7:24–25 (NIV)

door

"Laid off." The words were a slap in the face. I'd worked at the same job for nearly 40 years, and then one day I was told that I was no longer needed. I drove home in a daze.

Former colleagues shared leads to positions in my field. Some jobs looked beyond my reach, while others seemed like a step down.

What if I made the wrong choice?

My friend Paula suggested I claim the scripture Revelation 3:7 (see the next page) as the focus for my prayers and for my job search. "If it's the job God wants you to have, He'll open the door," she said. "If it's not, He'll slam that door shut."

I prayed the verse every day, asking God to open the door to the position He wanted me to have and close any doors I shouldn't enter.

Six months after losing my job, I received an offer and accepted it confidently, knowing God had unlocked the door for me.

—Beth Gooch

Dear Lord, please give me the courage to knock on the doors You put in front of me, knowing that You'll equip me for what lies ahead.

Words to Pray On

When he opens a door, no one can close it, and when he closes it, no one can open it.

—Revelation 3:7 (GNT)

Ask, and you will receive; seek, and you will find; knock, and the door will be opened to you. For everyone who asks will receive, and anyone who seeks will find, and the door will be opened to those who knock.

—Matthew 7:7–8 (GNT)

They must thank the Lord for his constant love, for the wonderful things he did for them. He breaks down doors of bronze and smashes iron bars.

—Psalm 107:15–16 (GNT)

stories

Happy sigh. I just finished reading a very good story. As I close the book, I nod and smile to myself, knowing I'll read it again someday.

I love stories, always have. I get caught up in the excitement as characters fight the enemy, or fall in love, or make their way to a new life. I grow through their experiences and learn through their mistakes. When the princess struggles, I'm her. And as the hero rescues her, I'm him too. The story and everything in it—the setting, the plot, the theme—become a part of me, and I'm better for it.

My life is a story, one God wrote at creation. As I face challenges and lean into the love of my hero Jesus, I look forward to the next chapter and the next after that, knowing that this story, like the stories of all believers, has a happy ending.

—Heidi Gaul

God, thank You for letting me be part of this bigger story called creation. May I do it justice. Amen.

Words to Pray On

God saw all that he had made, and it was very good.

—Genesis 1:31 (NIV)

Let the redeemed of the Lord tell their story—those he redeemed from the hand of the foe, those he gathered from the lands, from east and west, from north and south. Some wandered in desert wastelands, finding no way to a city where they could settle. They were hungry and thirsty, and their lives ebbed away. Then they cried out to the Lord in their trouble, and he delivered them from their distress....Let them give thanks to the Lord for his unfailing love and his wonderful deeds for mankind, for he satisfies the thirsty and fills the hungry with good things.

—Psalm 107:2–9 (NIV)

Acknowledgments

Every attempt has been made to credit the sources of copyrighted material used in this book. If any such acknowledgment has been inadvertently omitted or miscredited, receipt of such information would be appreciated.

Scripture quotations marked (CEB) are taken from the *Common English Bible*. Copyright © 2011 by Common English Bible.

Scripture quotations marked (CSB) are taken from *The Christian Standard Bible*, copyright © 2017 by Holman Bible Publishers. Used by permission.

Scripture quotations marked (ESV) are taken from *The Holy Bible, English Standard Version*. Copyright © 2001 by Crossway Bibles, a division of Good News Publishers. Used by permission. All rights reserved.

Scripture quotations marked (GNT) are taken from the *Good News Translation*® (Today's English Version, Second Edition) © 1992 American Bible Society.

Scripture quotations marked (HCSB) are taken from the *Holman Christian Standard Bible*. Copyright © 1999, 2000, 2002, 2003, 2009 by Holman Bible Publishers, Nashville, Tennessee. All rights reserved.

Scripture quotations marked (MSG) are taken from *The Message*. Copyright © 1993, 2002, 2018 by Eugene H. Peterson.

Scripture quotations marked (NASB) are taken from the *New American Standard Bible*®, Copyright © 1960, 1971, 1977, 1995, 2020 by The Lockman Foundation. All rights reserved.

Scripture quotations marked (NIV) are taken from *The Holy Bible, New International Version*®, NIV®. Copyright © 1973, 1978, 1984, 2011 by Biblica, Inc. Used by permission. All rights reserved worldwide.

Scripture quotations marked (NKJV) are taken from the *New King James Version*®. Copyright © 1982 by Thomas Nelson. Used by permission. All rights reserved.

Scripture quotations marked (NLT) are taken from the *Holy Bible, New Living Translation*. Copyright © 1996, 2004, 2007, 2015 by Tyndale House Foundation. Used by permission of Tyndale House Publishers Inc., Carol Stream, Illinois. All rights reserved.

Scripture quotations marked (TLB) are taken from *The Living Bible*. Copyright © 1971 by Tyndale House Publishers, Inc., Carol Stream, Illinois. All rights reserved.

A Note from the Editors

We hope you enjoyed *Pray a Word for Strength*, published by Guideposts. For over seventy-five years, Guideposts, a nonprofit organization, has been driven by a vision of a world filled with hope. We aspire to be the voice of a trusted friend, a friend who makes you feel more hopeful and connected.

By making a purchase from Guideposts, you join our community in touching millions of lives, inspiring them to believe that all things are possible through faith, hope, and prayer. Your continued support allows us to provide uplifting resources to those in need. Whether through our communities, websites, apps, or publications, we inspire our audiences, bring them together, and comfort, uplift, entertain, and guide them. Visit us at guideposts.org to learn more.

We would love to hear from you. Write us at Guideposts, P.O. Box 5815, Harlan, Iowa 51593 or call us at (800) 932-2145. Did you love *Pray a Word for Strength*? Leave a review for this product on guideposts.org/shop. Your feedback helps others in our community find relevant products.

Find inspiration, find faith, find Guideposts.
Shop our best sellers and favorites at
guideposts.org/shop
Or scan the QR code to go directly to our Shop

Printed in the United States
by Baker & Taylor Publisher Services